I'M A CHRISTIAN NOW!

THE LIFE OF JESUS

90-DAY DEVOTIONAL JOURNAL
WITH DAILY ACTIVITIES

ANNA SARGENT

LifeWay Press®
Nashville, TN 37234

Item 005810304

DEWEY: 242.62
SUBHD: CHILDREN--RELIGIOUS LIFE \ DISCIPLESHIP \ REGENERATION (CHRISTIANITY)

Printed in the United States of America

Kids Ministry Publishing
LifeWay Church Resources
One LifeWay Plaza
Nashville, Tennessee 37234-0172

We believe the Bible has God for its author; salvation for its end;
and truth, without any mixture of error, for its matter
and that all Scripture is totally true and trustworthy.

To review LifeWay's doctrinal guideline,
please visit *www.lifeway.com/doctrinalguideline.*

CONTENTS

Following Jesus is the most important decision you will ever make, because it changes everything! You are no longer in control of your life—Jesus is! You no longer do whatever you feel like—God guides you! Because Jesus is now Lord of your life, this book is meant to help you better understand who He is and how to follow Him. Here are a few things to keep in mind as you use it:

The Bible contains God's words to us. For this reason, we don't just read the Bible to become smarter; we read it to grow in our relationship with God. This is why we begin each devotion with the Verse of the Day. Pray before you read the Verse of the Day, and ask the Holy Spirit to help you understand what you read in your Bible. A Challenge Bible reference is also provided if you want to read more about the topic. Finally, you'll find a Family Devotion and a memory verse for each new section. Read these devotions with your family and try to memorize a memory verse each week. Check out all the memory verses on pgs. 102-103.

In addition to the Bible readings, each devotion includes four activities:

DO IT! gets your brain thinking about the topic of the day. Write or draw as much as you want there.

KNOW IT! gives you key facts from Scripture about the day's topic. Look up the Bible references to see where the key facts come from.

ASK IT! is a space for you to write a question you have after completing the devotion. Ask a parent, sibling, or Sunday school teacher these questions when you get a chance.

PRAY IT! offers simple suggestions for talking to God. It's a good idea to pray at the beginning and end of each devotion.

 Look for this symbol as you work through your journal. This symbol means it's time for a "Parent Talk!" You have reached a place where it would be good for your parents to read and discuss the information with you. When you see a Parent Talk symbol, take your journal to your parents and ask them to discuss it with you.

Remember, being a Christian means trusting in Jesus and having a relationship with God. It means making different decisions because Jesus is your Lord. It does *not* mean doing everything perfectly or being exactly like Jesus right away. When you mess up, God promises to forgive you (1 John 1:9), and as you grow in faith, God promises to make you more like Jesus (Philippians 1:6). God is thrilled that you are a Christian now! He is eager to reveal Himself to you and help you follow Jesus.

This book is set up for you to complete one devotion per day for six days, over the course of three months. This is the suggested pace, but you don't have to do it like this. You could do three devotions per week instead, or two devotions per day, if you like. The goal is not about the timeline; it's about spending regular time with Jesus so that you can learn to follow Him as a Christian.

As you complete each day, check it off in the chart below. Thank God for your progress as you mark off more and more days.

WEEK #	FAMILY DEVO	DAY 1	DAY 2	DAY 3	DAY 4	DAY 5	DAY 6

Dear Parents,

Jesus said, "Let the little children come to me, and do not hinder them, for the kingdom of heaven belongs to such as these." (Matthew 19:14, NIV) Consider this: Jesus is even more delighted than you are that your child is now following Him! He has sealed her with His Holy Spirit, given her spiritual gifts for contribution, and promised to be with her always. Your child can now come to the throne of grace freely and rest in the same promises of Scripture that you can. What a wonderful gift to celebrate!

As your child spends time in this devotional learning who Jesus is and what His life was like, you can best help her by doing the following:

Pray. The most important thing you can do is pray. Ask God to reveal Himself to your child through the daily Bible readings and challenge verses. Ask Him for guidance as you try to answer questions she brings up (James 1:5). Ask God to grow both of your relationships with Him, as well as your relationship with each other.

Model. Read your Bible and talk about it. Tell your children what God is up to in your own life and what you are learning from Him. Model what it means to depend on the Scriptures in the day to day (Deuteronomy 6:4-7).

Encourage. 90 days is a long time, so your child might grow weary in working all the way through this devotional. Ask her how it's going. Affirm her when she chooses to do devotions on her own. Emphasize that we all need encouragement from other Christians as we grow in our relationships with Jesus (Hebrews 3:13).

Be patient. Sanctification often happens slowly in your own life, and it's no different for your child. Remember that it's not your job to change your child's heart. God is the one who does the work of sanctification through the power of the Holy Spirit (2 Corinthians 3:18). When you grow weary in being patient with your child, ask God for strength and help in your time of need (Hebrews 4:16).

WHAT DO YOU KNOW?

Before you start Day 1, let's find out what you already know, and what you want to know, about the life of Jesus!

Q: WHAT ARE SOME THINGS YOU ALREADY KNOW ABOUT JESUS?

A:

Q: WHAT DO YOU HOPE TO LEARN ABOUT JESUS FROM THIS BOOK?

A:

Q: CIRCLE ALL THE FEELINGS YOU FEEL ABOUT STARTING THIS BOOK.

HAPPY	UNSURE
NERVOUS	EAGER
EXCITED	HOPEFUL

WHY DID YOU CHOOSE THOSE WORDS?

A:

JESUS THE ETERNAL GOD

Since you have this book, you probably already know some stories about Jesus. Stop and think of some of your favorites. What do those stories teach you about Jesus? What words would you use to describe who Jesus is?

Did you know that whatever you thought of has *always* been true about Jesus? For example, if you thought about a powerful miracle, Jesus has *always* been that powerful. Jesus brought that power from heaven with Him when He came to earth. Jesus will never lose His power, and He will always use it for good. Or maybe you thought about Jesus teaching people. Jesus brought that wisdom from heaven to earth. He has *always* been all-wise and able to teach the hearts of those who put their faith in God. Or maybe you thought about the story of Jesus' birth, where Mary laid Jesus in a manger and the shepherds came to worship Him. It was *always* God's plan for Jesus to come to earth as a baby. Jesus fully revealed the plan God always had to save people.

When we say Jesus *always* existed or something was *always* the plan, we're talking about Jesus' *eternal* nature. *Eternal* means "forever." Think about this: most things in our lives have a beginning and an end. Books have a starting page and a final page. Amusement parks have an opening time and a closing time. Songs have a first note and a last note. But Jesus is different. Jesus is eternal. Jesus always has been and always will be. That's because Jesus is God. Jesus left His throne in heaven to spend about 33 years on earth. When everything Jesus was supposed to do was finished, He went back to heaven, where He rules now and forever.

Because Jesus is the eternal God, when we look at Jesus, we see exactly what God is like. We see the things God cares about. We see what causes God to be angry, sad, or pleased. We see how much power God has and how He chooses to use it. We see how God responds to sin and how much He loves us.

As you dive into the eternal nature of Jesus, think about how it affects your life. If Jesus is eternal, then He is not limited by anything! Jesus sees all things, knows all things, and does all things perfectly. Jesus knew about your whole life before you were even born, and He has a plan for your life that fits into His bigger plan. Trust Him. Praise Him for having so much power. Worship Him for being eternal.

"I am the Alpha and the Omega, the first and the last, the beginning and the end." Revelation 22:13

DAY 1
THE WORD OF GOD

Verse of the Day: John 1:1-3

Challenge: John 1:4-14

 DO IT Write your answers to these questions.

How do you know if something or someone is real?

How do you know Jesus is real?

What would you tell a friend who asked you to prove Jesus is real?

 KNOW IT
★ Jesus is God (John 1:1-2).
★ Jesus has existed since the beginning of time (John 1:1-2).
★ Jesus was there when the world was created, and everything was created through Him (Colossians 1:15-17).

 ASK IT

 PRAY IT Worship Jesus for being God. Thank Him for creating the world and everything in it. Tell Jesus you believe He is real.

 PARENT Talk Watch a video or read a book together. Discuss the difference between what is real and true in the story and what is fiction.

DAY 2
THE PERFECT REFLECTION

Verse of the Day: Colossians: 1:15-23

Challenge: John 5:8-17

 DO IT Draw the reflection of the image opposite the dotted line.

 KNOW IT
★ Jesus and God the Father are one (John 10:30).
★ Everything Jesus said came from our heavenly Father (John 12:49).
★ When you look at Jesus, you can see what God is like (Colossians 1:15).

 ASK IT

 PRAY IT Worship Jesus for coming to earth and showing us what God is like. Thank Jesus for something you have learned about God through His life on earth.

9

DAY 3

THE BEGINNING AND THE END

Verse of the Day: Revelation 22:13

Challenge: Isaiah 46:10

DO IT — Think about the things you typically do in a day. Write four things along the timeline, keeping in mind whether or not they take place near the beginning, middle, or end of the day.

Beginning   Middle   End

KNOW IT
★ Jesus lives forever (Revelation 22:13). He knows all things (Hebrews 4:13).
★ His plan will always succeed (Isaiah 46:10).

ASK IT

PRAY IT — Worship Jesus for being eternal and knowing all things. Ask Him to help you trust that His plans are always good.

DAY 4

A THOUSAND YEARS AND A DAY

Verse of the Day: 2 Peter 3:8   Challenge: Psalm 40:5

KNOW IT
★ A thousand years are like one day to God. He exists outside of time (2 Peter 3:8).
★ God never grows tired, and He does not sleep (Psalm 121:4, Isaiah 40:28).
★ God does not change (Malachi 3:6).

DO IT — Circle the dots in groups of ten. How many more groups would you need to have 1,000 dots? Hint: Count by 100's

. . . .
. . . .
. . . .
. . . .
. . . .
. . . .
. . . .
. . . .

100 100 100 100 100 100
100 100 100 100 100 100

100 X _____ = _____

ASK IT

PRAY IT
★ Thank God for always being awake and available to hear your prayers. Worship God for being unchangeable, and for always being someone you can rely on.

DAY 5
TRILLIONS OF THOUGHTS

Verse of the Day: Psalm 139:17

Challenge: Psalm 139: 16-18

 Color the shells that look like this ☺ in blue and the shells that look like this 🐚 in yellow.

 ★ God has more thoughts about you than the number of sands on the seashore (Psalm 139:18).
★ God knows the number of hairs on your head (Luke 12:7).
★ God knows how many days you will live (Psalm 139:16).

 ASK IT

 ★ Thank God for thinking about you so much! Worship God for knowing things you cannot know, like how many hairs are on your head or how many days everyone will live. Tell Him you trust Him.

DAY 6
RIGHT TIME, RIGHT PLACE

Verse of the Day: Acts 17:26-27

Challenge: Psalm 139:13-16

 Fill out your passport. If you don't know all the information, ask your parents to help.

MY PASSPORT

ME

_____
TODAY'S DATE

_____
NAME

_____
DATE OF BIRTH

_____
PLACE OF BIRTH

 ★ God decided when and where you would live (Acts 17:26-27).
★ God put you where you are for a reason (Psalm 37:23).
★ Jesus came to earth at the perfect time to die for sinners. (Galatians 4:4).

 ASK IT

 ★ Thank God for putting you in your specific family, school, and neighborhood. Ask Him to help you share about Jesus in those places. Thank God for sending Jesus for us.

GENESIS   LEVITICUS   DEUTERONOMY

THE LAW

EXODUS

POETRY

PSALMS   ECCLESIASTES

JOB

SONG OF SONGS

ISAIAH   LAMENTATIONS

MAJOR PROPHETS

JEREMIAH

EZEKIEL

HISTORY

JOSHUA   JUDGES   1 & 2 SAMUEL   1 & 2 KINGS

MINOR PROPHETS

1 & 2 CHRONICLES

EZRA

ESTHER

HOSEA   JOEL   AMOS   OBADIAH   MICAH

NAHUM HABAKKUK ZEPHANIAH

ZECHARIAH MALACHI

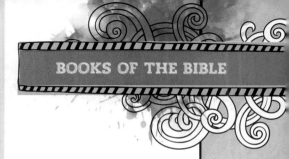

Look at the names of the books of the Bible. Fill in the names of the missing Bible books, then number the divisions in the correct order, beginning with "The Law."

The 39 books of the **Old Testament** tell the story of God's chosen people, the Israelites. The books describe the promised Messiah, who is necessary to restore people's relationship with God.

The **New Testament's** 27 books tell how Jesus—the Messiah—came to fulfill what was written in the Old Testament and give instructions about following Him!

THE GOSPELS

    JOHN

MATTHEW   LUKE

1 & 2 CORINTHIANS

   PHILIPPIANS

PAUL'S LETTERS

OMANS   GALATIANS   1 & 2 TIMOTHY

     PHILEMON

COLOSSIANS

1 & 2 THESSALONIANS

PROPHECY   **HISTORY**   ACTS

REVELATION

GENERAL LETTERS

1, 2, & 3 JOHN

      JUDE

HEBREWS   1 & 2 PETER

JESUS IN THE OLD TESTAMENT

If a friend were to ask you to describe the Old Testament, what would you say? Would you say it is the first part of the Bible? Would you mention some popular stories from the Old Testament, like Adam and Eve or David and Goliath? You might say that the Old Testament tells us about things that happened before Jesus was born.

What if your friend asked you to describe the New Testament? Would you say that it tells about Jesus' life, death, and resurrection? Would you talk about the stories that happened after Jesus returned to heaven, like the missionary adventures of Paul and Peter, or teachings like the armor of God?

All of these answers would be correct, but not completely true. While the Bible is divided into Old and New Testaments, it is actually ONE story: the story of God's relationship with us through Jesus.

While the name "Jesus" is not found in the Old Testament, God talked about Him and gave many hints about His coming before He was born. In fact, right after Adam and Eve sinned, God promised to send someone to crush Satan (Genesis 3:15). Through Old Testament prophets like Isaiah, God repeatedly said He would send a Messiah, or "Savior" into the world. He described what the Messiah would be like and declared what He would do (Isaiah 7, 9, 53, 61).

It's important to know that the ONE story of the Bible has always been about Jesus so that we can better understand who God is. God didn't change His plan between the Old and New Testaments. The stories you read in the Old Testament about God rescuing His people when they didn't deserve it were all there for a reason. They were all pointing to the ultimate way God would save us: through Jesus.

The truth is, whether you lived during Old Testament or New Testament times, a relationship with God has always been built on faith. In the Old Testament, Jesus had not yet come, but people could put their faith in the God who promised to send Jesus. Today, we can put our faith in the God who has already sent Jesus. Either way, people are saved by faith in the God whose plan for our salvation was always about Jesus.

As you study this topic, think about how the prophecies you read were written over a thousand years before Jesus lived! Worship God for knowing all things in the past, present, and future. Praise Him for giving the prophets many messages about Jesus. Thank Him for the gift of salvation we can have through faith.

"For a child will be born for us, a son will be given to us, and the government will be on his shoulders. He will be named Wonderful Counselor, Mighty God, Eternal Father, Prince of Peace." Isaiah 9:6

DAY 1
GOD'S PLAN FROM THE BEGINNING

Verse of the Day: Genesis 3:14-15, 17-18

Challenge: Galatians 4:4-7

 DO IT The story in Genesis 3 is real and true, and it's much more exciting than what we find in comic books. In the space below, draw your own pictures showing what Genesis 3:14 and 3:17-18 say will happen as a result of Adam and Eve's sin.

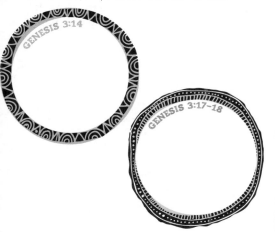

GENESIS 3:14

GENESIS 3:17-18

 KNOW IT ★ God knows everything. He knew Adam and Eve would sin by disobeying Him (Psalm 147:5).
★ God always had a plan to deal with sin. That plan was to send Jesus (Ephesians 1:4).
★ Jesus came to earth to die for our sins and be raised from the dead so we could be saved (Romans 10:9-10).

 ASK IT

 PRAY IT Thank God that He always had a plan to send Jesus. Thank Jesus for coming to earth to die for sin so we can live forever with God.

DAY 2
THE OLD TESTAMENT TELLS ABOUT GOD'S PLAN

Verse of the Day: Isaiah 9:6-7

Challenge: Isaiah 11:1-5

 DO IT A plan is "knowing what you want to do in the future." Circle the pictures that represent things you plan to do or places you plan to go this week.

Sometimes our plans get interrupted, but God's plans never do. When the time was right, God sent His Son Jesus into the world. This plan was perfect.

 KNOW IT ★ Since before creation, God's plan was to be with us through Jesus (Ephesians 1:4).
★ Many prophets in the Old Testament told about God's plan to send Jesus (Luke 24:44).
★ When you become a Christian, Jesus is always with you (Matthew 28:20).

 ASK IT

 PRAY IT Ask God to help you trust His plans, since they are always good and happen in His perfect timing. Thank God for His greatest plan to give us Jesus.

15

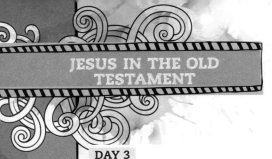
DAY 4
THE OLD TESTAMENT TELLS ABOUT JESUS' WORK

Verse of the Day: Isaiah 61:1-2

Challenge: Luke 4:16-21

 DO IT Draw faces on the three people below. The first is a guilty person who has just been forgiven. The second is a sick person who has been healed. The last is a lonely person who has just heard about Jesus.

What do all of these faces have in common? Why did you draw them the way you did?

 KNOW IT ★ Jesus read a prophecy from the Book of Isaiah that was about the Messiah (Luke 4:16-21).
★ The prophet Isaiah told what the Messiah would do when He came to earth (Luke 4:18-19).
★ Jesus told the people that Isaiah was talking about Him. Jesus is the Messiah (Luke 4:20-21).

ASK IT

 PRAY IT Praise Jesus for being strong enough to heal our bodies and our hearts. Praise God for sending prophets to proclaim Jesus' coming long before He arrived.

DAY 3
THE OLD TESTAMENT TELLS ABOUT JESUS' BIRTH

Verse of the Day: Micah 5:2

Challenge: Matthew 1:1-6

 DO IT Ask your mom or dad to help you answer these questions about where you were born:

_____

What city/town were you born in?

_____

What state were you born in?

_____

What country were you born in?

_____

If you were born in a hospital, what is the hospital's name?

_____

If you weren't born in a hospital, where were you born?

 KNOW IT ★ Jesus' ancestors (older family members) included Abraham, Ruth, Boaz, and King David (Matthew 1:1-6).
★ Ruth and Boaz lived in Bethlehem, a town near Jerusalem. David was anointed king in Bethlehem too (Ruth 4:11, 1 Samuel 16:18).
★ About 700 years before Jesus was born, the prophet Micah said Jesus would be born in Bethlehem (Micah 5:2).

ASK IT

 PRAY IT Thank God for loving you so much to send His Son Jesus to be born in Bethlehem. Praise God for planning this long before it happened and for delivering the message through His prophet Micah.

DAY 5

THE OLD TESTAMENT TELLS ABOUT JESUS' DEATH AND RESURRECTION

Verse of the Day: Psalm 16:8-11

Challenge: Isaiah 53:4-10

 DO IT Color in all the 1's in the grid below to reveal a special name.

Jesus is special because, as God's Son, He is the only person who could pay for sin by dying and rising again.

2	2	1	7	2	3	4	5	2	6	7	8	7	9	2	8	4	5	4
6	6	1	3	1	1	9	1	1	1	5	1	6	1	7	1	1	1	
4	4	1	9	1	6	1	8	1	9	4	2	1	2	1	6	1	2	5
7	7	1	5	1	1	1	8	1	1	1	2	1	3	1	4	1	1	1
1	4	1	6	1	8	4	9	3	2	1	3	1	4	1	5	6	6	1
1	1	1	8	1	1	1	3	1	1	1	5	1	1	1	8	1	1	1

 KNOW IT ★ King David wrote about the promise of the Messiah's resurrection from the dead (Psalm 16:8-11; Acts 2:25-33).

★ The prophet Isaiah wrote the Messiah would suffer, die for our sins, and be raised back to life (Isaiah 53:4-10).

★ Jesus' death was not an accident. Jesus willingly gave up His life for us to follow God's plan (John 10:18).

ASK IT

 PRAY IT Worship God for revealing His plan of Jesus' death and resurrection long before it happened. Praise Jesus for coming to carry out God's plan.

DAY 6

ALL OLD TESTAMENT STORIES ARE POINTING TO JESUS

Verse of the Day: Luke 24:27

Challenge: Luke 24:44-49

 DO IT Using colorful markers or pens, draw different kinds of arrows (squiggly, zig zag, dotted, thick, etc.) all around Jesus. Make sure the pointed tip is facing Him.

 KNOW IT ★ Every command and prophecy God gave in the Old Testament later came true through Jesus (Matthew 5:17).

★ Jesus said the entire Old Testament was about Him (Luke 24:27).

★ The people in the Old Testament could never perfectly obey God's law. Every person sins so every story in the Old Testament shows us our need for Jesus (Romans 3:10).

ASK IT

 PRAY IT Thank God for showing you your need for Jesus. Thank Him that the Bible is all about Jesus, your Savior and Lord. Ask Him to help you understand how Jesus fulfills everything written in the Old Testament.

JESUS

1 Born in Bethlehem

2 Worshiped by the shepherds

3 Greeted by Simeon and Anna in the temple

13 Walked on water

11 Healed Jairus' daughter

12 Fed the 5,000

14 Healed 10 men with a skin disease

17 Entered Jerusalem triumphantly

16 Visited Zacchaeus

15 Blessed the children

24 Appeared to many people

25 Cooked breakfast for disciples

26 Ascended to heaven

PARENT Talk

Work together with your parent to find as many Scripture references to the timeline of Jesus in the Gospels.

5 Learned at the temple

6 Baptized by John

4 Visited by the wise men

7 Tempted by Satan

9 Preached the Sermon on the Mount

10 Calmed a storm

8 Called the first disciples

18 Had the Last Supper with the disciples

19 Prayed in Gethsemane

20 Arrested and tried

23 Resurrected: Jesus is alive!

22 Buried in a tomb

21 Died on a cross

JESUS, THE BABY AND THE BOY

Sometimes it's hard to believe anybody understands you, isn't it? Maybe you're going through something difficult at school or something confusing at home. When you look around, you think, "Nobody else has to deal with this. Nobody else understands."

This week we'll see that Jesus understands everything we go through. He understands our emotions, our fears, our struggles, and our temptations to sin. Not only does Jesus understand adults, but He also understands kids too, because He was a kid once!

Think about this: Jesus is God. He could have come to earth the first time any way He wanted. The Bible tells us when Jesus returns to earth in the future, He will come from heaven to establish His kingdom forever. Jesus could have come to earth like this before, or He could have appeared on earth as a grown man.

So why did Jesus come to earth as a *baby*? Have you been around a baby recently? All babies do is eat, sleep, cry, and eat, sleep, and cry some more. They are totally helpless and dependent on their parents to take care of them. Why did Jesus choose to go through this? Why did Jesus choose to have a childhood? Why did He live in a family, with a mom and dad, brothers and sisters, and chores and responsibilities?

Jesus did all of this so that He could understand what our lives are like. Jesus knows what it's like to have a sibling bug Him or a mom tell Him to go do His chores. He knows what it's like to sit down and learn from someone older. Jesus might not have gone through your exact circumstances, but He understands your feelings because He experienced them once too. He knows what it's like to feel young or misunderstood, and He has felt every possible emotion— from happiness to anger, from sadness to hope.

Jesus also faced every temptation to sin. He was tempted to lie and deceive, take what was not His, hurt those who hurt Him, and talk badly about people. But every single time Jesus had a choice to make, He chose to honor God. Every single time He could have given into sin, He didn't. This is why when you are tempted to sin, you can ask Jesus for help. He understands what you are dealing with, and He can help you overcome it.

This week, as you study Jesus' childhood, remember that He does understand what you are going through. Talk to Him about the hard things that are going on in your life. Ask Him for help overcoming a particular sin. Don't think you have to wait until you are older to get serious about this. God wants to hear about everything you're dealing with *right now*. He understands you and will be right there to help you.

"And Jesus increased in wisdom and stature, and in favor with God and with people." Luke 2:52

DAY 1
MARY AND JOSEPH HEARD FROM ANGELS

Verses of the Day: Luke 1:30-31
Matthew 1:20-21

Challenge: Luke 1:26-38 / Matthew 1:18-25

 DO IT Ask your mom or dad what it was like when they found out you were going to be born.

Did an angel speak to them? Did someone help you understand that you were "on the way"? Put these details about the birth of Jesus in the right order by numbering the events 1-5. Read Luke 1:26-38 if you need help.

_____ Mary said, "I am the Lord's servant; let it be as you say."

_____ The angel Gabriel told Mary that she would have a son.

_____ Mary was confused and worried about this sudden news, but she had faith in God.

_____ The angel Gabriel appeared to a young Jewish woman named Mary.

_____ Mary was told to name the baby Jesus, and He would be the Son of God.

 KNOW IT ★ God chose Mary and Joseph to be Jesus' parents here on earth (Matthew 1:20-21).
★ Jesus' birth seemed impossible to Mary and Joseph, but nothing is impossible with God (Luke 1:37).
★ Mary and Joseph obeyed God and were willing to be part of His plan (Luke 1:38, Matthew 1:24).

ASK IT

PRAY IT Praise God for fulfilling His plan to send Jesus. Thank God for the example that Mary and Joseph set, and ask Him to help you trust His plans as Mary and Joseph did.

DAY 2
JESUS WAS BORN

Verse of the Day: Luke 2:7-16

Challenge: Luke 2:1-20

 DO IT Think about these things: Have you ever stayed in a hotel? What was it like? If you haven't stayed in a hotel, what do you think it would be like? How does it make you feel to know that God's Son Jesus was born where the animals were kept, because there was no room for them in the inn?

In the space below, draw a manger, or feeding trough for animals, that would have been Jesus' bed.

 KNOW IT ★ Mary gave birth to Jesus among the animals in a stable. Then she laid the baby Jesus in a manger, or feeding trough (Luke 2:7).
★ The angel told the shepherds the good news about Jesus' birth. He said this good news was for all the people (Luke 2:10).
★ The shepherds found Jesus lying in the manger, just as the angel had said (Luke 2:16).

ASK IT

PRAY IT Worship Jesus for coming to earth as a baby. Praise God for the good news of the birth of Jesus, which is for all people.

DAY 3
JESUS WAS DEDICATED

Verse of the Day: Luke 2:28-30

Challenge: Luke 2:21-38

 DO IT In the blocks going down, write the name of each picture. Read the letters across the top of the blocks to discover another name Jesus is called.

 KNOW IT ★ Mary and Joseph named their baby Jesus, just as the angel had told them to (Luke 2:21).

★ As part of Jewish law, every firstborn male was dedicated to the Lord. Mary and Joseph dedicated Jesus (Luke 2:23).

★ Mary and Joseph did not tell Simeon who Jesus was. The Holy Spirit did (Luke 2:27-28).

ASK IT

 PRAY IT Thank God for making it clear to Simeon that Jesus was the Messiah, or promised Savior. Thank God for making the same thing clear to you. Pray for a friend that does not yet believe in Jesus, that they will know who He truly is.

DAY 4
WISE MEN VISITED JESUS

Verse of the Day: Matthew 2:1-2

Challenge: Matthew 2:3-12

 DO IT The wise men brought gifts to Jesus. What gifts can you give to Jesus? Follow the path below. On each box, write one gift you can give to Jesus.

START

FINISH

 KNOW IT ★ Wise men from eastern countries saw a star in the sky and followed it to find Jesus (Matthew 2:1-2).

★ The wise men brought Jesus gold, frankincense, and myrrh, which were precious gifts (Matthew 2:11).

★ God used the wise men to protect Jesus from King Herod (Matthew 2:12).

ASK IT

 PRAY IT Praise God for sending someone to tell you about Jesus so you can worship Him. Ask God to give you a heart that would gladly give your greatest treasures to Jesus.

DAY 5
JESUS GREW UP

Verse of the Day: Luke 2:40, 52

Challenge: Isaiah 53:1-3

 DO IT Cross out all the odd-numbered letters. Write the remaining letters in order in the spaces below to discover one of Jesus' names.

I	Z	H	M
M	A	T	I
S	B	N	U
W	E	K	O
R	U	L	N

___ ___ ___ ___ ___ ___ ___ ___
2 8 22 14 4 42 38 26

Immanuel means "God with us." Jesus came to live among us. He was born as a baby and grew up just like you and me.

 KNOW IT
★ Immanuel means "God with us" (Matthew 1:23).
★ Jesus knows what it's like to be a kid and grow up (Luke 2:52).
★ Jesus understands everything you're going through, so you can talk to Him about anything (Hebrews 4:15).

ASK IT

 PRAY IT Tell Jesus something hard that you're going through right now. Remember that Jesus was a kid once too, so you can trust Him to understand and ask Him for help.

DAY 6
JESUS LEARNED IN THE TEMPLE

Verse of the Day: Luke 2:46-47

Challenge: Luke 2:41-51

 DO IT Mary and Joseph searched for Jesus for three days before they found Him in the temple.
Find the following words in the word search below: Jesus, Mary, Joseph, three, temple, Jerusalem, teachers, questions, learn

P	E	F	C	Z	M	S	I	M	I	J	N
Q	V	I	N	D	X	N	E	Z	Y	O	I
E	K	N	I	G	M	L	W	V	I	S	N
N	D	T	C	J	A	A	X	I	I	E	P
R	Q	U	E	S	T	I	O	N	S	P	J
A	U	X	U	A	D	W	Z	D	D	H	T
E	Z	R	I	M	C	M	S	U	S	E	J
L	E	H	S	R	C	H	X	Q	M	T	I
J	Z	R	Y	N	E	E	E	P	M	C	F
Z	M	R	H	G	V	J	L	R	D	A	K
H	A	Q	W	T	D	E	N	T	S	E	K
M	G	C	A	O	X	H	G	Q	K	R	R

 KNOW IT
★ God the Father is Jesus' *true* Father (John 16:28).
★ As a boy, Jesus wanted to know about His Father more than anything else (Luke 2:46).
★ Jesus did not sin by staying in the temple. Jesus was fulfilling God's plan to grow in wisdom (Luke 2:49, 52).

ASK IT

 PRAY IT Tell Jesus you believe He knows what being a kid is like. Ask Him for guidance as you learn and grow up too. Praise Him for being the perfect Son of God.

A genealogy is "a study of a person's line of ancestors (people in his family)." Read Matthew 1:1-16 and fill in the blanks with the missing names to learn about Jesus' genealogy.

(NOTE: Some Bible translations spell the names differently.)

FROM ABRAHAM TO DAVID

_____ fathered Isaac,

Isaac fathered Jacob,

Jacob fathered _____,

_____ fathered Perez,

Perez fathered Hezron,

Hezron fathered _____,

_____ fathered Amminadab,

Amminadab fathered Nahshon,

Nahshon fathered Salmon,

Salmon fathered _____,

_____ fathered Obed,

Obed fathered Jesse,

and Jesse fathered _____.

FROM DAVID TO THE BABYLONIAN EXILE

_____ fathered Solomon,

Solomon fathered Rehoboam,

Rehoboam fathered Abijah,

Abijah fathered _____,

_____ fathered Jehoshaphat,

Jehoshaphat fathered Joram,

Joram fathered _____,

_____ fathered Jotham,

Jotham fathered Ahaz,

Ahaz fathered Hezekiah,

Hezekiah fathered _____,

_____ fathered Amon,

Amon fathered Josiah,

and Josiah fathered Jechoniah.

FROM THE EXILE TO THE MESSIAH

Jechoniah fathered _____,

_____ fathered Zerubbabel,

Zerubbabel fathered Abiud,

Abiud fathered Eliakim,

Eliakim fathered _____,

_____ fathered Zadok,

Zadok fathered Achim,

Achim fathered Eliud,

Eliud fathered _____,

_____ fathered Matthan,

Matthan fathered Jacob, and

Jacob fathered _____

the husband of _____,

who gave birth to _____

who is called the Messiah.

Do you know who your ancestors are? Start by filling in the box at the bottom of the tree with your name, then add your parents' names and their parents' names (your grandparents).

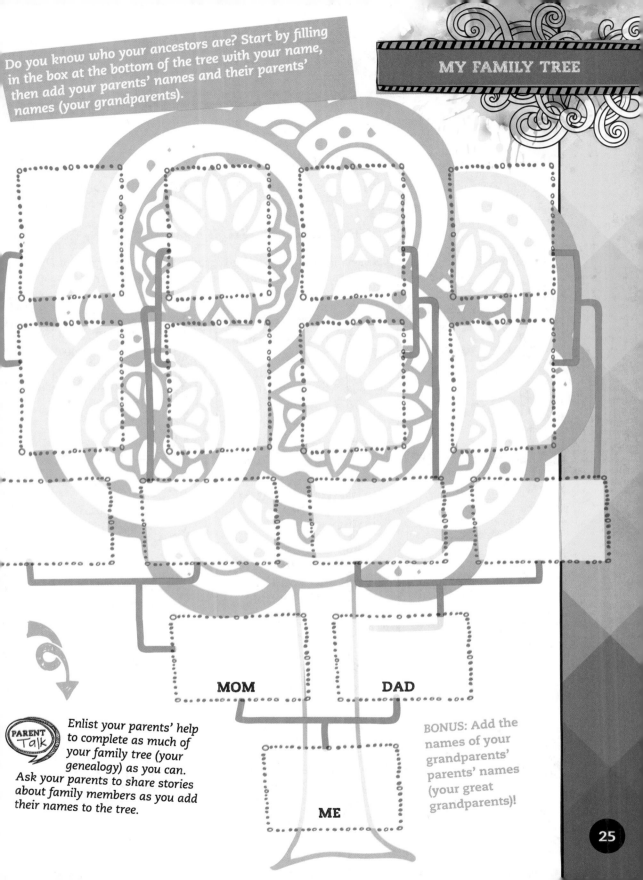

MOM

DAD

PARENT Talk Enlist your parents' help to complete as much of your family tree (your genealogy) as you can. Ask your parents to share stories about family members as you add their names to the tree.

ME

BONUS: Add the names of your grandparents' parents' names (your great grandparents)!

REMEMBER THE STORY

When reading a Bible story as a family, ask the following questions about the Bible passage.

WHO, WHERE, WHAT?

Note: Sometimes you cannot find every answer. If that's the case, don't make an answer up! These questions are simply to help you remember the details of the story better.

WHO are the people in the story?

WHERE are the people in the story? What does their location have to do with what happens?

WHAT are the people saying? What are they doing? What stands out?

HOW AND WHY?

HOW do you think the people in this story were feeling?

WHY do you think the people made the decisions they did?

WHY do you think this story is in the Bible?

"Listen, Israel: The Lord our God, the Lord is one. Love the Lord your God with all your heart, with all your soul, and with all your strength. These words that I am giving you today are to be in your heart. Repeat them to your children. Talk about them when you sit in your house and when you walk along the road, when you lie down and when you get up."
Deuteronomy 6:4–7

DIG DEEPER

After reading, retell the story to one another. Next, review the story with the following questions:

What did you learn about **PEOPLE**?

What do you **LEARN** about God in the story?

What did you **LIKE** about what we read?

Is there anything that **CONFUSED** you?

Is there anything that **UPSET** you?

Was there **AN EXAMPLE** to follow?

Was there a sin **TO AVOID**?

What should we talk to God about **AFTER** reading this story?

Were there **COMMANDS** we need to obey?

Was there **A PROMISE OF GOD** to trust in?

JESUS, THE SON OF GOD

For most of Jesus' life, He was a single man living in a small town called Nazareth, working as a carpenter. But God the Father had a special plan for Jesus: to show His love, tell His truth, demonstrate His power, and die for sinners. So when Jesus was about 30 years old, it was time for Jesus' ministry to begin. But *how?*

God had planned for a special messenger named John the Baptist to prepare the way for Jesus (Matthew 3:1-3). John invited people to repent of their sins and be baptized in the Jordan River. To "repent of sin" means to turn away from sin and turn to God. To be *baptized* is to be lowered underwater and come back up as a public sign that you have repented of sin and trusted in Jesus. Many people asked John to baptize them. *Even Jesus.*

This confused John the Baptist. Why would Jesus be baptized? He was the perfect Son of God. He had never sinned! When Jesus came to the Jordan River, John the Baptist said, "Jesus, you need to baptize *me*, not the other way around!" (Matthew 3:14)

John the Baptist was right. Well, sort of. Jesus was perfect and didn't need to repent of sin. Instead, Jesus was baptized at the beginning of His ministry to hint at what was coming at the end of His ministry. Going under water hinted at Jesus' death. Coming back up out of the water hinted at Jesus' resurrection.

Today, being immersed under water and brought back up in baptism is not just a sign that we have been forgiven of our sins. It also shows the world *why* we are forgiven: we have put our faith in Jesus, who died and was raised back to life!

After Jesus came up out of the water, the Holy Spirit descended from heaven like a dove and God the Father spoke, saying, "This is my beloved Son with whom I am well pleased" (Matthew 3:17). Everyone who was at the Jordan River that day heard this. God the Father had declared that Jesus was His Son! The question now was: *What would the Son of God do?*

The first thing Jesus did was *go away.* He went into the desert, where He fasted for 40 days. After that, Satan came to tempt Jesus. Three times Satan tempted Him, and three times Jesus resisted his temptations using the Scriptures. In doing this, Jesus proved Himself again to be the perfect Son of God.

For the next three years, Jesus' ministry amazed people, surprised people, and confused people. We'll spend most of this devotional digging into what His ministry was like, what it shows us about God, and why it matters for you now that you're a Christian!

"And a voice from heaven said: 'This is My beloved Son, with whom I am well-pleased.'" Matthew 3:17

DAY 1
THE WAY OF THE LORD

Verse of the Day: John 14:6

Challenge: Matthew 3:1-11

 DO IT Find your way through the maze to get to John the Baptist at the Jordan River.

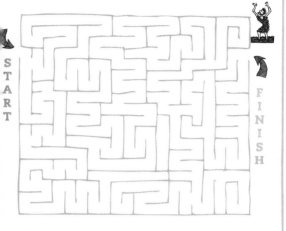

There is only one way to make it through this maze. Jesus said He is the way, the truth, and the life. No one comes to God except through Him.

 KNOW IT ★ John the Baptist was God's special messenger who baptized people and prepared the way for Jesus (Matthew 3:3).
★ John the Baptist said he was not even worthy to untie Jesus' sandals (Matthew 3:11).
★ Jesus Christ is the only way to God (John 14:6).

 ASK IT

 PRAY IT Thank God for sending John the Baptist to prepare the way for Jesus. Worship Jesus for being the Son of God who made a way for us to enter the kingdom of heaven.

DAY 2
JESUS WAS BAPTIZED

Verse of the Day: Mark 1:9

Challenge: Matthew 3:13-17

 **DO IT** Circle the places you like to swim.

Baptism and swimming are different. Swimming is about fun and exercise. In baptism, a person is immersed in water and brought up again to show that she has trusted in Jesus and she now lives to follow Jesus.

 KNOW IT ★ Baptism is a public declaration of faith in Jesus. It is an act and being put under water and brought back up to tell others in the church that you have trusted in Jesus (Romans 6:3-4).
★ Jesus was baptized even though He never sinned. When a person is baptized, he is following Jesus' example (Matthew 3:14-15).
★ Baptism does not *make* a person a Christian but *shows* others she has become a Christian (Matthew 28:19).

 ASK IT

 PRAY IT Thank Jesus for setting the example in baptism even though He never sinned. Thank Him for the opportunity to know and follow Him. If you have not been baptized, ask God to make it clear to you when to be.

DAY 3
JESUS WAS TEMPTED WITH FOOD

Verse of the Day: Deuteronomy 8:3

Challenge: Matthew 4:1-4

 DO IT Place a checkmark by all the things you would eat.

What things did you not place a checkmark by? Why not? Why could you not eat stones?

Jesus had not eaten food for 40 days. Satan knew Jesus was hungry, so he tempted Jesus to turn the stones into bread. Jesus easily could have done this. Instead, Jesus quoted Deuteronomy 8:3 that says "man does not live by bread alone."

 KNOW IT
★ To *tempt* means "to try to get someone to sin."
★ To *fast* means to not do something for a certain amount of time so that you can spend more time with God. God cannot be tempted and will not tempt anyone (James 1:13).
★ With God's help, you can avoid giving into temptation (1 Corinthians 10:13).

 ASK IT

 PRAY IT Thank Jesus for resisting every temptation and for helping us fight temptation too. Thank Him for the reminder that we need more than food to live . . . we need God's Word too.

DAY 4
JESUS WAS TEMPTED TO TEST GOD

Verse of the Day: Deuteronomy 6:16

Challenge: Matthew 4:5-7

 DO IT Did you know you can test your sense? Draw a line from the place on the girl's face to the object that would help test that sense.

SONG

FLOWER

RAINBOW

LEMON

What sense is not listed on the page?

How can you test your sense of touch?

How did Satan tempt Jesus to test God's faithfulness?

 KNOW IT
★ The Bible says to not test God, but to trust and obey Him (Deuteronomy 6:16-17).
★ Jesus used Scripture to fight against temptation (Matthew 4:7).
★ If you memorize Scripture, God can bring those words to mind when you are tempted (Psalm 119:11).

 ASK IT

 PRAY IT Ask God to help you memorize Scripture so that you can be prepared when temptation comes. Praise Jesus for fighting every temptation and never sinning.

DAY 5
JESUS WAS TEMPTED WITH POWER

Verse of the Day: Deuteronomy 6:13

Challenge: Matthew 4:8-11

DO IT In the box below, draw what you would do if you could rule the world for a day.

Ruling the world seems like it would be awesome. Maybe your first rule would be no homework for a whole month for every kid. Or maybe it would be free cake for everyone the morning of their birthday. Whatever rules you came up with, ruling over that many people is a lot of power! Hopefully you would use that power to do good!

KNOW IT ★ Satan offered Jesus everything God planned to give Him, but without suffering (Matthew 4:9).
★ Jesus trusted God's plan for His life most of all (Luke 22:42).
★ Jesus resisted Satan's temptations by trusting in the Word of God (Matthew 4:10).

ASK IT

PRAY IT Praise Jesus for being God's perfect Son who resisted every temptation. Confess a temptation you have given into recently. Ask God to help you trust His words more than anything else.

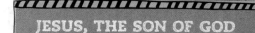
DAY 6
FIGHTING SIN

Verse of the Day: Philippians 4:13

Challenge: Proverbs 28:6-10

DO IT Jesus used Scripture to help Him fight the temptation to sin. Read the verses and match them to a temptation they might help you resist.

When you are tempted to:	Read this:
• Talk back to your parents	• Matthew 6:19-21
• Eat too much	• Proverbs 11:13
• Gossip about a friend	• Proverbs 23:20-21
• Store up money for yourself	• Deuteronomy 5:16
• Cheat on a test	• Leviticus 19:11

The Bible is full of verses that will help you know what to do when facing temptation.

KNOW IT ★ Everybody is tempted to sin, and everybody will sin (Romans 3:10).
★ Sin hurts us and destroys us (Proverbs 14:11-12).
★ If we confess our sins, God is faithful and just to forgive us (1 John 1:9).

ASK IT

PRAY IT Tell God about a sin you are struggling with. Ask Him for Bible verses that would help you fight that sin. Thank Him for forgiving your sins when you do give into temptation.

JESUS' BAPTISM

Draw a picture of what you think Jesus' baptism looked like. Use John 3:13-17 if you need help.

WHEN JESUS WAS BAPTIZED:

WHERE JESUS WAS BAPTIZED

WHO BAPTIZED JESUS:

HOW DO YOU THINK JESUS FELT AFTER BEING BAPTIZED?

If you have already been baptized, draw a picture of your baptism. (Or ask your parents for a picture of your baptism and tape it inside the frame.)

PARENT Talk Talk about why it is important to be baptized. Read Matthew 28:18-20 together. What commands did Jesus give His disciples?

WHEN I WAS BAPTIZED:

WHERE I WAS BAPTIZED:

WHO BAPTIZED ME:

HOW I FELT AFTER BEING BAPTIZED:

WHO WATCHED ME BE BAPTIZED:

JESUS THE LEADER

The dictionary defines a *leader* as "someone who leads or commands a group." Most of the leaders in your life are probably adults. For example, the leader of your classroom is the teacher, and the leader of your school is the principal. If you are on a sports team, your leader is the coach. If you are in a band or orchestra, the leader is the conductor. Can you think of any other leaders in your life? What makes your favorite leaders so great? God puts leaders in our lives to train us, guide us, and correct us when we are going down the wrong path. He gives us good leaders so we have someone to look up to, or someone we want to become like.

When Jesus started His ministry on earth, it quickly became clear He was a *leader*. Many people were drawn to Him, His teachings, and His miracles. Mark 1:22 tells us, "They were astonished at his teaching because he was teaching them as one who had authority, and not like the scribes." And John 6:2 says, "A huge crowd was following him because they saw the signs that he was performing by healing the sick."

Still, Jesus didn't want people following Him just because of what He could teach or do. He wanted people to follow Him because of who He was: the Son of God who had come into the world to save sinners and change their lives. Jesus said when you follow Him, He becomes the leader of your *whole life*. This was hard for people to understand, and it's why many who followed Jesus in the beginning of His ministry left Him later on.

When you become a Christian, Jesus becomes the leader of *your whole life*, not just in the parts that are easy to give Him. Christians follow Jesus' words in *everything*: in family, friendships, money, belongings, time, talents, and more.

Following Jesus' leadership in everything is hard for us, because we like being the leaders of our own lives. We prefer to make our own rules, listen to our own thoughts, and do our own thing. Becoming a Christian means following Jesus as your leader, because You know He is God's Son who died for you, so you trust Him.

Remember when you pictured your favorite leaders and what made them so great? Jesus is an even better leader than the best leaders you know. Jesus is the best because His decisions are always 100% good, right, and true. Remember that God gives us leaders to train us, guide us, and steer us down the right paths. Jesus will always do this perfectly. When you follow after Jesus, God promises that you will become more like Him (Philippians 1:6, 2 Corinthians 3:18). So keep on following all the leaders God has given you, and above all, follow Jesus.

"For you were called to this, because Christ also suffered for you, leaving you an example, that you should follow in his steps."
1 Peter 2:21

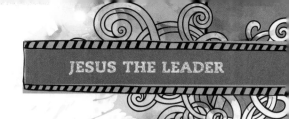

DAY 1
SEEK GOD'S KINGDOM FIRST

Verse of the Day: Matthew 6:33

Challenge: Matthew 6:19-21

 DO IT Rank your top 3 places to go, foods to eat, and things to do for fun.

	PLACES	FOODS	FUN
1			
2			
3			

Favorite things are often good gifts from God. When Jesus is the leader of your life, He will become more important than any of your favorite things.

 KNOW IT ★ Jesus said if we seek God's kingdom first, we will receive everything we need from God (Matthew 6:33).
★ Sometimes seeking God's kingdom means giving up things that are important to us (Matthew 4:22).
★ Jesus is worth giving everything up for (Philippians 3:8).

 ASK IT

 PRAY IT Thank God for sending Jesus to be more important than any of our favorite things. Ask Him for help seeking His kingdom first.

DAY 2
OBEY JESUS' WORDS

Verse of the Day: Matthew 7:24-27

Challenge: John 14:23-24

 DO IT Complete the dot-to-dots.

 KNOW IT ★ A foundation provides support and strength for a house.
★ Jesus said His words are like a solid foundation of our lives (Matthew 7:24).
★ Jesus said His words will never pass away (Mark 13:31).

ASK IT

 PRAY IT Thank God for giving humans the Bible. Ask Him for help to understand His words and for guidance in how to build your life on them.

DAY 3
FOLLOW JESUS' EXAMPLE

Verse of the Day: John 13:12-17

Challenge: Hebrews 12:1-2

 DO IT Match these Bible verses to the correct description of Jesus.

JESUS

★ showed humility → John 13:14-15

★ served others → John 8:55

★ glorified God → Philippians 2:5-8

★ obeyed God → Mark 1:35

★ spent time with → John 17:4
   God and prayed

 PARENT Talk Take turns washing each other's feet. Talk about the experience. Now imagine your family members' feet had been covered in dirt. Talk about how Jesus washed His disciples' dirty feet to set the example for how we should serve others.

 KNOW IT ★ Christians seek to live as Jesus did (1 John 2:6).
★ Jesus said we should follow His example of serving others (John 13:14).
★ When we learn from Jesus as our leader, we will find rest (Matthew 11:29).

ASK IT

 PRAY IT Thank Jesus for coming into the world to set an example for how to live. Think of one way you want to live like Jesus more and ask God for help with that.

DAY 4
TAKE UP YOUR CROSS

Verse of the Day: Matthew 16:24-25

Challenge: Matthew 16:26-28

 DO IT What is the heaviest thing you can lift? Ask permission, then go around your house and try to lift some of these things:

Were you able to lift these things? Now imagine trying to carry one of these heavy things on your back. Do you think you could do it? Jesus said following Him is like carrying a cross on your back every day. Jesus was crucified on a cross. Crosses are heavy and not easy to carry!

 KNOW IT ★ Sometimes following Jesus is really hard (John 16:33).
★ Even though following Jesus is hard, He promises to be with us (Matthew 28:20).
★ Following Jesus is always worth it in the end (Matthew 16:25).

ASK IT

 PRAY IT Thank Jesus for dying on a cross to save us from our sins. Ask Him for help following Him as your leader, even when it's hard.

DAY 5
FISH FOR PEOPLE

Verse of the Day: Matthew 4:18-20

Challenge: Matthew 4:17-23

 DO IT Circle ten fish with stripes in the picture below.

 KNOW IT ★ Jesus invited fishermen to "fish for people" along with Him (Matthew 4:19).

★ To "fish for people" means to tell people everywhere the good news about Jesus (Acts 1:8).

★ When we tell people the good news, we trust that God is the one who saves them (1 Corinthians 3:6-7).

ASK IT

 PRAY IT Thank God for inviting you to be a "fisher of people" too. Ask Him for boldness to share the good news of Jesus with family, friends, and neighbors.

 PARENT Talk Ask your parents to share an example of a time they listened to the Holy Spirit and obeyed. How did they know it was the Holy Spirit, and not just their own thoughts or desires?

DAY 6
LISTEN TO THE HOLY SPIRIT

Verse of the Day: John 14:26

Challenge: John 16:7-15

 DO IT Stop and listen. Write down all the sounds you can hear right now, even if they are faint. Do you hear sounds from outside? Sounds from inside? Are these familiar sounds? Are these soothing sounds?

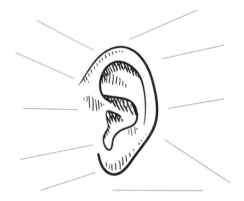

When we listen to the Holy Spirit, we are not usually listening for a voice like a human voice. Instead, we are hearing God speak to us within our spirit.

 KNOW IT ★ The Holy Spirit helps us remember Jesus' words (John 14:26).

★ Ignoring the Holy Spirit makes God sad (Ephesians 4:30).

★ The Holy Spirit helps us understand the Bible (1 Corinthians 2:12).

ASK IT

 PRAY IT Thank God for giving you the Holy Spirit. Ask for help listening to the Holy Spirit.

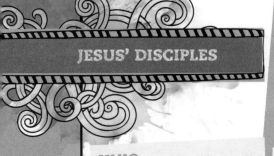

Unscramble the letters in the boxes below to discover the names of Jesus' disciples. Write the names in the spaces. If you need help, read the Bible verses or check out Matthew 10:2-4.

HNJO

---

was a fisherman on the Sea of Galilee with his father Zebedee and his brother, James. Jesus called him to be a disciple while he was repairing nets (Matthew 4:21-22). He helped Peter prepare the Passover meal (Luke 22:8). From the cross, Jesus told him to care for His mother (John 19:26-27).

SUJAD RTICSOAI

---

was the keeper of the disciples' money bag. He betrayed Jesus for 30 pieces of silver (Matthew 26:15). He was sorry for what he had done and hanged himself (Matthew 27:3-5).

AHMSOT

---

encouraged the disciples to go with Jesus and die with Him (John 11:16). He wanted proof that Jesus had risen from the dead (John 20:25). Jesus showed him His hands and side to prove His resurrection (John 20:27).

The Bible tells nothing about

MJSAE

---

except that he was the son of Alphaeus. (Matthew 10:3)

DDAAETUSH (Mark 3:18).

(OR JDSUA)

---

asked Jesus how He was going to reveal Himself to the disciples and not to the world (John 14:22).

SJEAM

---

was a fisherman on the Sea of Galilee with his father Zebedee and his brother, John. Jesus called him to be a disciple while he was repairing nets (Matthew 4:21-22). He was the first disciple to be killed for his faith.

Jesus called

TTAWEMH

---

to be a disciple while he was a tax collector in Capernaum. He invited his friends to a dinner where they could meet Jesus (Matthew 9:9-13).

WBEARMOTLOH

(OR AAAELTNHN)

---

was invited to see Jesus by Philip. Jesus called him a "true Israelite" (John 1:45-51).

Jesus called
HPIILP

---

to follow Him as a disciple (John 1:43). He found Nathanael and told him about Jesus (John 1:43-45). He went with Andrew to bring some Greeks to Jesus (John 12:20-22).

The Bible tells us nothing about

OIMSN the Zealot

---

except for his name (Matthew 10:4).

WAEDRN

---

was a fisherman with his brother, Simon Peter, on the Sea of Galilee. Jesus called him to be a disciple while he was fishing (Matthew 4:18-20). He brought his brother, Simon Peter, to Jesus (John 1:40-42), and told Jesus about the boy with the loaves and fishes (John 6:8-9).

NIOSM EERPT

---

was a fisherman with his brother, Andrew, on the Sea of Galilee. Jesus called him to be a disciple while he was fishing (Matthew 4:18-20). Jesus helped him walk on water (Matthew 14:29). He denied Jesus before His crucifixion (Luke 22:54-62) and was later forgiven by Jesus (John 21:15-19).

Check out some of Jesus' commands! Fill in the blanks by Reading the Scripture verses, then Use the Missing Words to complete the crosshord puzzle.

DOWN
1. _____ your parents (Matthew 15:4).
2. Make and baptize _____ (Matthew 28:19).
5. Love your _____ (Matthew 22:39).
6. Ask, _____ , knock (Matthew 7:7-8).
7. _____ the Lord (Matthew 22:37).
8. _____ Me (Matthew 4:19).

ACROSS:
3. _____ to God (Matthew 11:15).
4. Love your _____ (Matthew 5:44).
9. _____ others (Matthew 18:21-22).
10. Seek first the _____ of God (Matthew 6:33).
11. Do not _____ (Matthew 7:1).
12. Do not _____ about your life (Matthew 6:25).

WORD BANK:

FOLLOW   DISCIPLES   LOVE
LISTEN   HONOR   KINGDOM
SEEK   ENEMIES   NEIGHBOR
FORGIVE   JUDGE   WORRY

39

JESUS THE TEACHER

We learned last week that Jesus was a popular leader and taught many people. Part of this was because Jesus said things that no one had heard before. In Matthew 5-7, the disciple Matthew recorded one of Jesus' teachings called the Sermon on the Mount. Here are some of the surprising things Jesus said during that sermon:

★ People who are the most blessed, or "happy in God," are those who are lowly, gentle, and persecuted for God.
★ We should love our enemies and pray for those who hurt us.
★ We should be generous, even when someone takes us for granted.
★ We should not brag when we give generously to others.
★ We should not judge other people before we judge ourselves.
★ We should not worry about anything.

In this sermon, Jesus was explaining what it means to follow God. He was reminding the people that following God doesn't mean just doing the right things. In fact, He pointed out that no one could *ever* do all the right things (Matthew 5:20). Instead, Jesus taught that following God meant doing right things from a heart that completely trusts in God. Following God meant doing the right thing even when it didn't make sense, or even if you don't get recognition for it.

You see, the people were used to following God's rules, but many of them—especially the religious leaders—were doing so from a wrong heart. They were trying to make themselves look good before God and others. But that's not the point of obeying God. We obey God to make *God* look good, because we love Him so much. During the Sermon on the Mount, Jesus commanded, "Let your light shine before others, so that they may see your good works and give glory to your Father who is in heaven" (Matthew 5:16). Does the glory for your good works go to you? No, it goes to God.

Obedience starts with our love for God and love for others, not with trying to make ourselves look good. This love grows the more we spend time with God, the more we ask forgiveness for our sins, and the more we depend on Him in the day-to-day things. In any case, there's no point in trying to make ourselves look good before God. God already knows we are all sinners in need of saving! That's why He sent Jesus. Our only job as Christians is to show the world there is a God who loves us, and that we can do the right thing out of love for Him.

"Love the Lord your God with all your heart, with all your soul, and with all your mind. This is the greatest and most important command. The second is like it: Love your neighbor as yourself."
Matthew 22:37-39

DAY 1
THE BEATITUDES

Verse of the Day: Matthew 5:3-11

Challenge: Philippians 2:5-11

 DO IT Find the "Attitude to Be" that corresponds with the "Beatitude" and write the letter beside it. If you need help, ask a parent to do the activity with you.

BEATITUDE

___ 1. Poor in spirit

___ 2. Mourn

___ 3. Gentle or meek

___ 4. Hunger and thirst for righteousness

___ 5. Merciful

___ 6. Pure in heart

___ 7. Peacemaker

___ 8. Persecuted for righteousness

ATTITUDES TO BE

A. Focus on the beauty and truth of God

B. Submit to God and consider others before myself

C. Stand strong in faith, even when others make fun

D. Desire God's way more than my own

E. Be aware of my sin and my need for God

F. Forgive others because I have been forgiven

G. Be truly sad over my sin

H. Help others get along

 PARENT Talk Memorize the Lord's prayer as a family. Practice saying it once a day together over the next week. Take turns saying the prayer out loud at meals, bedtime, etc.

 KNOW IT ★ It is impossible to live out the Beatitudes without God's help (Ezekiel 36:27).
★ Those who live this kind of life Jesus described are blessed (Matthew 5:3-11).
★ To be *blessed* is to be happy in God.

ASK IT

PRAY IT Thank Jesus for preaching on the Beatitudes. Choose one of the Beatitudes you need the most help with right now. Ask the Holy Spirit to help you with that Beatitude this week.

DAY 2
THE LORD'S PRAYER

Verse of the Day: Matthew 6:9-13

Challenge: Matthew 6:5-8

 DO IT Each box of the Lord's Prayer below stands for something Jesus prayed for. Color in each box to match what it represents. Help and Protection–Blue; Dependence–Green; Praise–Yellow; Obedience–Purple; Forgiveness–Red.

Our Father in heaven, Your name be honored as holy.

Your kingdom come. Your will be done on earth as it is in heaven.

Give us today our daily bread.

And forgive us our debts, as we also have forgiven our debtors.

And do not bring us into temptation, but deliver us from the evil one.

For Yours is the kingdom and the power and the glory forever. Amen.

 KNOW IT ★ Jesus said you can talk to God anytime (Matthew 6:9-13).
★ Prayer is one key way to build your relationship with God (1 Thessalonians 5:17).
★ As you pray, you will become more aware of all the ways God provides for you (Psalm 143:5).

 ASK IT

 PRAY IT Pray a prayer of praise. Ask for help and protection from something. Repent of a sin you committed this week. Ask God to help you obey and tell others about Jesus.

41

DAY 3
LOVE YOUR ENEMIES

Verse of the Day: Matthew 5:43-48

Challenge: Matthew 5:38-48

 DO IT Write the initials of people in each of the places below who may have hurt you and you need to pray for.

MY CHURCH

MY NEIGHBORHOOD

MY SCHOOL

 KNOW IT
★ Jesus loved and prayed for those who treated Him terribly (Luke 23:34).
★ Jesus said we also should love and pray for those who treat us badly (Matthew 5:44).
★ You cannot say you love God and hate other people (1 John 4:20).

ASK IT

 PRAY IT Tell God if there is a person you have a hard time loving. Confess your sin if you have hated that person in your heart. Ask God to give you a heart like Jesus, who loved and prayed for those who treated Him terribly.

DAY 4
NO NEED TO WORRY

Verse of the Day: Matthew 6:25-26

Challenge: Matthew 6:25-34

 DO IT Jesus said the flowers and birds don't worry about what to wear or eat, because God takes care of them. He loves you much more than flowers and birds, so you know He'll take care of you!

Write on the petals of the flower or the feathers of the bird things you are worried about. Color in the petals or feathers until the picture is complete.

 PARENT Talk Take turns sharing something you are worried about. Pray for God to give everyone in your family peace and wisdom. When you are worried, take your concerns to God and give Him thanks (Philippians 4:6).

 KNOW IT
★ God may not give you what you want, but He promises to give you what you need (Matthew 6:33).
★ Worrying can be a sign that your heart does not trust God (Isaiah 26:3).

ASK IT

 PRAY IT Thank God for hearing your prayers. If you are worried about something, tell Him what it is. Ask Him to give you peace of mind. Before ending your prayer, thank God for two things in your life.

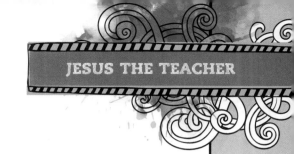
DAY 5

THE GREATEST COMMANDMENT

Verse of the Day: Mark 12:28-30

Challenge: Deuteronomy 6:4-8

 DO IT Jesus said the greatest commandment is to love the Lord your God with all your heart, mind, soul, and strength.

Find the following words in the word search below: greatest, commandment, heart, mind, soul, strength, love, God, first.

G	H	B	E	E	M	X	Z	L	Y	T
X	R	V	L	W	T	Z	L	M	F	X
V	O	E	E	B	X	M	L	K	S	Z
L	Q	A	A	U	C	N	U	T	T	P
W	F	I	F	T	X	I	O	J	R	H
R	P	I	O	S	E	Y	S	H	E	U
N	T	G	A	D	Y	S	E	P	N	U
T	S	R	I	F	N	A	T	L	G	S
G	O	D	N	P	R	I	S	C	T	V
L	A	B	U	T	M	H	M	W	H	H
C	O	M	M	A	N	D	M	E	N	T

 KNOW IT
★ Christians love God because He loved us first (1 John 4:19).
★ The greatest commandment is the hardest commandment to follow (Romans 3:11).
★ Following the greatest commandment will bring you joy (1 Peter 1:8-9).

ASK IT

 PRAY IT Worship God for His great love. Admit to Him that you cannot follow the first commandment in your own strength, but that you want to follow it.

DAY 6

THE SECOND GREATEST COMMANDMENT

Verse of the Day: Mark 12:31

Challenge: Matthew 7:12

 DO IT Draw concentric hearts in the space below. **Concentric** means to draw one shape inside the other, like the circles below.

 KNOW IT
★ Jesus said to love your neighbor (Mark 12:31).
★ Jesus said to treat others the way you would like to be treated (Matthew 7:12).
★ To love your neighbors is to serve them, even if it costs you a lot (John 15:13).

ASK IT

 PRAY IT Tell God whom you are having trouble loving right now. Ask for forgiveness if you have hurt that person, and ask for help forgiving them if they hurt you.

PALESTINE
IN THE TIME OF JESUS

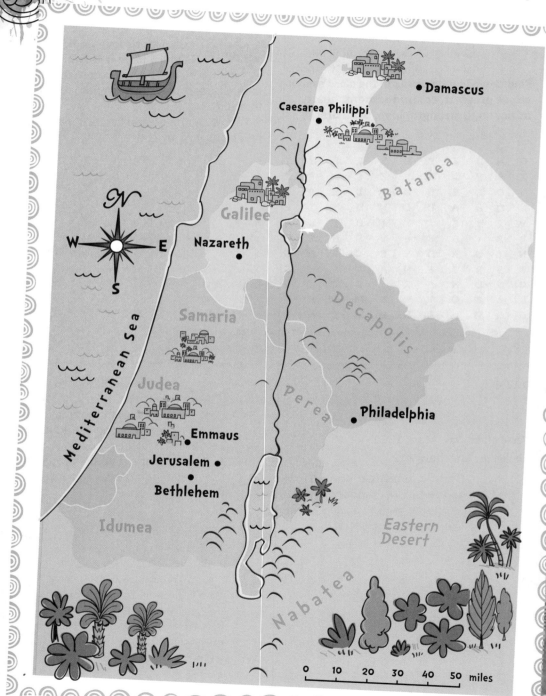

Damascus

Caesarea Philippi

Batanea

Galilee

Nazareth

Decapolis

Samaria

Perea

Judea

Philadelphia

Emmaus

Jerusalem

Bethlehem

Mediterranean Sea

Idumea

Eastern Desert

Nabatea

0 10 20 30 40 50 miles

JESUS' MINISTRY
AROUND THE SEA OF GALILEE

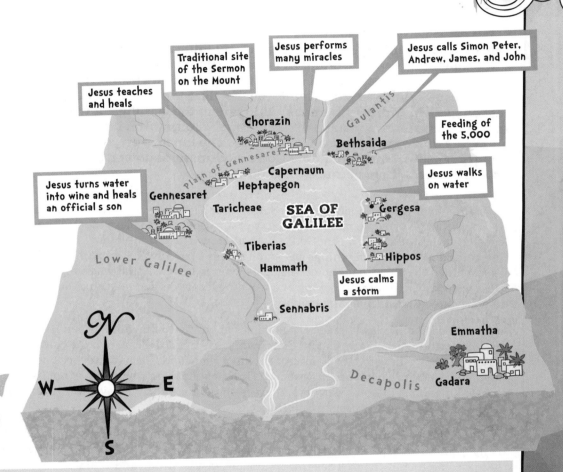

Traditional site of the Sermon on the Mount

Jesus performs many miracles

Jesus calls Simon Peter, Andrew, James, and John

Jesus teaches and heals

Feeding of the 5,000

Jesus turns water into wine and heals an official s son

Jesus walks on water

Jesus calms a storm

Chorazin

Gaulantis

Bethsaida

Plain of Gennesaret

Capernaum

Heptapegon

Gennesaret

Taricheae

SEA OF GALILEE

Gergesa

Tiberias

Hippos

Lower Galilee

Hammath

Sennabris

Emmatha

Decapolis

Gadara

Read the following Bible verses. Write the names of the places mentioned in the verses. Find the places on the maps and touch the names with your finger.

Matthew 2:1 _____

Matthew 15:29 _____

Matthew 4:13 _____

Matthew 16:13 _____

Matthew 14:34 _____

Matthew 21:1 _____

JESUS THE MIRACLE WORKER

During Jesus' ministry, He performed many miracles. A *miracle* is when God does something in our world that is impossible or that cannot be explained. Some of the miracles you will study this week include Jesus walking on water, Jesus calming a storm, and Jesus feeding thousands of people with just one lunch. Ordinary humans could not do these things! If we tried to walk on water, we would sink. If we spoke to a storm, it would keep on raging. If we gave thousands of people one lunch, everyone would go hungry. These miracles required God's supernatural power, and Jesus was able to perform them because He is God's Son.

As you study these miracles, keep in mind that Jesus was not putting on a show or trying to make Himself popular. Instead, Jesus used miracles to show the people what God is like, to give people more reason to worship God, and to bless them. Through Jesus' miracles, people saw that God is both all-powerful *and* all-loving. They saw that God cares deeply about big things *and* small things in our lives. For example, when Jesus calmed the storm so that His disciples wouldn't drown, that was a big thing. When Jesus turned water into wine at a wedding, that was a small thing. Both miracles demonstrated God's power and love.

Jesus also used miracles to teach His disciples about God's kingdom. When His disciples couldn't catch any fish on their own, Jesus filled their nets to the brim. When they didn't know how to feed a hungry crowd of thousands, Jesus fed every one of them with one little boy's lunch. Jesus was proving that God's kingdom is not like our earthly kingdoms. In God's kingdom, there is abundance and we have everything we need because we have access to God Himself.

Finally, Jesus performed miracles to prove He was God's Son. His greatest miracle was rising from the dead, and once the disciples saw that miracle with their own eyes, there was no turning back! They understood Jesus was strong and could do anything, they understood He was perfect and would always do the best thing. So after Jesus went back to heaven, His disciples continued to ask Him through His Holy Spirit to do miracles in their lives, and He often said yes (Acts 3:1-11, Acts 12:7-17, Acts 28:7-9).

Jesus is still alive and performing miracles today through the Holy Spirit. You can pray for Jesus to do things that cannot be explained, things you could never do on your own. Pray for Jesus to act in big ways and small ways, since you know He cares deeply about everything going on in your life. Nothing is impossible for Jesus, and He will always do the best thing. Whatever His answer to your prayers, Jesus remains all-powerful, all-loving, and always worthy of your worship.

"These are written so that you may believe that Jesus is the Messiah, the Son of God, and that by believing you may have life in his name." John 20:31

DAY 1
CHANGING WATER TO WINE

Verse of the Day: John 2:7-11

Challenge: John 2:1-12

DO IT Jesus performed His first miracle at a wedding. Read each word below aloud. Write a wedding-related word that rhymes on the line beside it. (example: side – bride).

* BROOM _____

* BAKE _____

* FLING _____

* MISS _____

* PRESS _____

Jesus' first miracle shows that God likes to bless us with good things at unexpected times.

PARENT Talk Ask your parents if they have ever had to rely on God to provide for them when it comes to work, food, health, family, or anything else. If there is something your family currently needs provision for, pray together for that the rest of the week.

KNOW IT ★ Jesus had the power to perform miracles because He is the Son of God (John 13:3).
★ Jesus has power over all of nature (Colossians 1:17).
★ Jesus did not perform miracles to show off, but to point people to God (John 2:9-11).

ASK IT

PRAY IT Praise God for His reign over the whole earth. Praise Jesus for His miracles, which proved He was the Son of God. Thank God for blessing us with good things at unexpected time.

JESUS THE MIRACLE WORKER

DAY 2
FILLING THE NETS

Verse of the Day: Luke 5:1-6

Challenge: John 21:1-11

DO IT Jesus commanded Peter to let out his fishing nets to catch some fish. Although Peter had not caught any fish all night, he obeyed Jesus and threw the nets out again. Read Luke 5:6. How would you explain what happened?

See how fast you can complete this maze.

START   FINISH

KNOW IT ★ Jesus is the Creator of all things, including the fish in the sea (John 1:1-3).
★ The fish came into the nets because every creature on earth belongs to God and obeys Him (Psalm 50:10-11).
★ Jesus performed this miracle to show He is the Son of God (Luke 5:8-11).

ASK IT

PRAY IT Praise God for ruling over all the creatures of the earth. Thank Jesus for using this miracle to show just how powerful He is. Ask the Holy Spirit for reminders of Jesus' power this week.

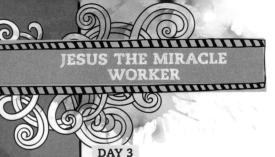

DAY 3
FEEDING THOUSANDS

Verse of the Day: John 6:8-13

Challenge: Matthew 15:32-39

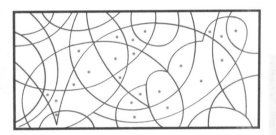 Five thousand men, plus women and children, had gathered to see Jesus! They were hungry, so Jesus decided to feed them. Color the dots to reveal what the people were fed.

Jesus fed the people fish and bread. Read John 6:9.

How many fish did Jesus have? _____

How many loaves of bread did Jesus have?

_____

Read John 6:13. How much food was left over? _____

KNOW IT ★ Jesus cares about the physical needs of people (John 6:11).
★ Christians need to care about people's physical needs too (James 2:15-17).
★ God provided more food than necessary to demonstrate His power and love (John 6:13).

ASK IT

PRAY IT Thank Jesus for showing us that God cares about our physical needs. Ask God to show you how you can meet someone's physical needs this week.

DAY 4
WALKING ON WATER

Verses of the Day: Matthew 14:25, 29

Challenge: Matthew 14:22-33

DO IT Fill a bowl or pan with water and place these items into the water: coin, spoon, leaf, rock, bar of soap, crayon, straw. Which items floated? Which items sank?

FLOATED: | **SANK:**

KNOW IT ★ Jesus could walk on water because He is the Son of God (Matthew 14:33).
★ Nothing is too hard for God (Jeremiah 32:17, 27).
★ Nothing is impossible for God (Matthew 19:26).

ASK IT

PRAY IT Praise God that He is able to do the impossible. Worship Jesus for having the power to walk on water and for letting Peter experience that power. Is there something you need to rely on God's power for today? Ask God to strengthen you.

PARENT Talk Four of the miracles that we've discussed this week include water. Play water games outside or do water experiments together. Talk about how Jesus has control over all of the earth's water, including all the oceans and the precipitation in the sky.

DAY 5
CALMING THE SEA

Verse of the Day: Luke 8:24

Challenge: Luke 8:22-25

 DO IT Use the picture of the boat to help you draw the same boat in the empty grid.

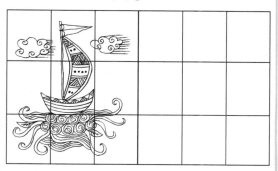

The weather on the Sea of Galilee is unpredictable, which means it changes all the time. Life can be like that too. How do you feel when unexpected things happen or plans change?

 KNOW IT ★ The disciples were afraid of the terrible storm (Luke 8:24).
★ Jesus was never afraid of the storm, because He trusted God perfectly (Luke 8:25).
★ Fully trusting in God helps us not be afraid as well (John 14:1).

 ASK IT

 PRAY IT Tell God about a personal struggle. Are you having a hard time in a friendship? At school? At home? Like the disciples did, go to Jesus with your worry and fear. Pray for more faith.

DAY 6
RAISING TO LIFE

Verse of the Day: John 11:43-44

Challenge: Mark 5:21-24, 35-43

 DO IT Write the names of the items. Write the highlighted letters in the spaces to solve the puzzle.

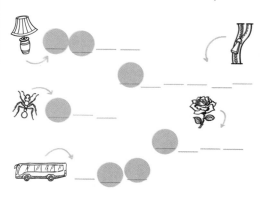

Jesus raised ___ ___ ___ ___ ___ ___ ___ from the dead.

Jesus raised people from the dead—young and old. Jesus was a close friend of Lazarus. The Scripture says Jesus loved Lazarus, so why did Jesus wait until Lazarus died to help him? Read John 11:41-42.

 KNOW IT ★ The just payment for sin is death (Romans 6:23).
★ Jesus said that anyone who believes in Him will live, even after she dies (John 11:25).
★ When Jesus died and rose again, He destroyed the power of death and the devil (Hebrews 2:14).

 ASK IT

 PRAY IT Are you afraid of death? If so, tell God how you feel. Then worship Jesus for being stronger than death and for giving you the hope of eternal life with Him forever in heaven.

MIRACLE STORIES IN THE GOSPELS

The first four books of the New Testament—Matthew, Mark, Luke, and John—are called the "Four Gospels." The Gospels tell about the life of Jesus. You can read about many of the miracles Jesus performed in more than one of the Gospels.

5,000 PEOPLE FED

★ Matthew 14:15-21
★ Mark 6:35-44
★ Luke 9:12-17
★ John 6:5-14

STORM CALMED

★ Matthew 8:23-27
★ Mark 4:35-41
★ Luke 8:22-25

DEMONS SEN INTO PIGS

★ Matthew 8:28-3
★ Mark 5:1-20
★ Luke 8:26-39

JAIRUS' DAUGHTER RAISED

★ Matthew 9:18-19,23-26
★ Mark 5:22-24,35-43
★ Luke 8:41-42,49-56

SICK WOMAN HEALED

★ Matthew 9:20-22
★ Mark 5:25-34
★ Luke 8:43-48

PARALYTIC MAN HEALED

★ Matthew 9:1-8
★ Mark 2:1-12
★ Luke 5:17-26

LEPER HEALED

★ Matthew 8:1-4
★ Mark 1:40-45
★ Luke 5:12-15

PETER'S MOTHER-IN-LAW HEALED

★ Matthew 8:14-15
★ Mark 1:29-31
★ Luke 4:38-39

SHRIVELED HAND RESTORED

★ Matthew 12:9-13
★ Mark 3:1-5
★ Luke 6:6-10

BOY WITH EVIL SPIRIT HEALED

★ Matthew 17:14-18
★ Mark 9:14-27
★ Luke 9:37-42

JESUS WALKED ON WATER

★ Matthew 14:22-33
★ Mark 6:45-52
★ John 6:16-21

GIRL FREED FROM DEMON

★ Matthew 15:21-28
★ Mark 7:24-30

BLIND MEN RECEIVE SIGHT

★ Matthew 20:29-34
★ Mark 10:46-52
★ Luke 18:35-43

CENTURION'S SERVANT HEALED

★ Matthew 8:5-13
★ Luke 7:1-10

FIG TREE CURSED

★ Matthew 21:18-22
★ Mark 11:12-14,20-24

JESUS THE STORYTELLER

Do you enjoy listening to someone tell a good story? What is one story recently that made you laugh? Made you cry? Made you think? Can you remember these stories well enough to retell them? Did you learn something important from any of these stories?

Did you know Jesus told lots of stories while He was on earth? God loves it when we use our imagination. Imagination helps us step outside of our own point-of-view and into someone else's to better understand an idea. Unlike some storytellers you might know, however, Jesus didn't primarily tell stories to entertain people. He told stories to illustrate deeper truths about God and His kingdom. These stories were really important because they helped people understand God's truth in a unique way. Jesus' special stories were called *parables*.

One of Jesus' parables goes something like this: "A farmer went out into his fields to plant seeds. Some of the seeds fell on the path, and the birds came by and ate them all. Some fell on rocky ground and were scorched by the sun. Some fell among thorns, which choked them before they grew. Finally, some of the seeds took root in good soil and grew into healthy plants."

If you were just passing by and heard Jesus teaching, you might think, *Wow, Jesus knows a lot about farming and how important it is for seeds to be planted properly*. That would be true, but the main reason Jesus was sharing this parable was to illustrate a deeper truth about God's kingdom.

Jesus later explained this parable to His disciples. He said that each soil represents different people who hear God's truth. Some people will never understand it (seed eaten by the birds); some people will accept God's truth, but when suffering comes, they'll turn away (seed on rocky ground); some people will hear God's truth but let other things become more important to them (seed among thorns); and some people will believe God's truth, let it take root in their hearts, and be fruitful in God's kingdom (seed on good soil). Jesus knew His disciples would understand the meaning of this parable because they believed in Him.

As you study some of Jesus' parables this week, ask Him to help you understand the meaning behind them. If you enjoy drawing, take the time to draw the scenes from each parable to help you remember the details. Ask God to teach you about Himself and His kingdom through these stories. Ask Him to show you what these parables mean for your life today. Spend time praising Jesus for using special stories to help you understand God's truth.

"Jesus told the crowds all these things in parables. . .so that what was spoken through the prophet might be fulfilled"
Matthew 13:34-35

DAY 1
THE GOOD SAMARITAN

Verse of the Day: Luke 10:25-37

Challenge: Deuteronomy 6:5;
Leviticus 19:18

 DO IT Write the name of the person(s) from the Bible story (Luke 10:25-37) each statement describes.

Asked how he could have eternal life.

Asked what the law said.

Asked, "Who is my neighbor?"

Told a parable.

Robbed and left on the side of the road.

Refused to help the hurt man.

Helped the hurt man.

Said, "Go and do the same thing."

 KNOW IT ★ It is not enough to know the right thing to do; you also have to do it (James 2:17-18).
★ Loving your neighbor means loving people that are different from you (Luke 10:36-37).
★ Loving others means taking care of their needs, even if you have to make sacrifices (Philippians 2:3-4).

 ASK IT

 PRAY IT Thank Jesus for teaching in parables so you can understand God's truths in new ways. Ask God if there's anybody in particular He wants you to sacrifice for this week.

DAY 2
THE LOST SON

Verse of the Day: Luke 15:11-32

Challenge: Romans 8:38-39

 DO IT Complete the maze so that the lost son can find his way home.

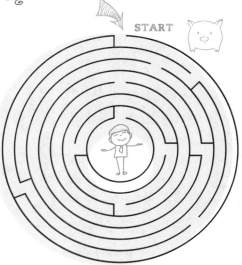

START

 KNOW IT ★ God is like the father in the parable, full of grace and mercy for His children (Luke 15:20).
★ Nothing in all the universe can separate Christians from the love of God (Romans 8:38-39).
★ Whenever you sin, God is faithful to forgive you because of Jesus (1 John 1:9).

ASK IT

 PRAY IT If you feel like the lost son from the parable in any way, tell God you want to change course and come back to Him. Thank God for the love and forgiveness He offers you in Jesus.

DAY 3
THE LOST SHEEP

Verse of the Day: Matthew 18:10-14

Challenge: John 10:7-18

 DO IT Count the sheep on the page. How many can you find? _____

How would you feel if you owned 100 sheep, but could only find 99? Would you leave the 99 to go find the one?

 PARENT Talk Invite everyone in the family to talk about a time they lost something. Ask each other, "How did you feel when you found out you lost it? Did you go searching for it? What did you do when you found it? What did you do if you didn't find it?"

 KNOW IT ★ Jesus is like a good shepherd, and you are like one of His sheep (John 10:11).

★ God will always seek after you when you try to run away from Him (Matthew 18:14).

★ God protects you, provides for you, and helps you through dark times (Psalm 23).

ASK IT

 PRAY IT Thank God for being a good shepherd and taking care of you.

DAY 4
THE TALENTS

Verse of the Day: Matthew 25:14-30

Challenge: Luke 19:12-27

 DO IT Read Matthew 25:14-30. Do the math to find out how much money each person received.

5 GIVEN
+ 5 EARNED
+ 1 EXTRA
_____

2 GIVEN
+ 2 EARNED
+ 0 EXTRA
_____

1 GIVEN
+ 0 EARNED
− 1 EXTRA
_____

How did the master respond to each person? List the talents and abilities God has given you.

If you don't know what those are, ask your parents, teachers, or other trustworthy adults.

 KNOW IT ★ In the parable, the word *talents* mean money (Matthew 25:14).

★ In your life, the word *talents* means anything God has blessed you with to give back to His kingdom (skills, abilities, character qualities, belongings, etc.).

★ God wants Christians to use their talents to help expand His kingdom (Matthew 25:21).

ASK IT

 PRAY IT Is there a talent you have that you want to start using in God's kingdom? Pray and ask God for opportunities to do so. Ask God to help you use your talents for His glory, not your own.

DAY 5
THE UNMERCIFUL SERVANT

Verse of the Day: Matthew 18:21-35

Challenge: Matthew 6:15

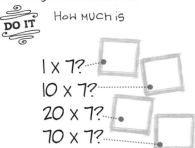

 DO IT How much is

1 x 7?

10 x 7?

20 x 7?

70 x 7?

When Peter asked Jesus how many times he had to forgive the same person, Jesus said 70 times 7 times, or almost 500 times. The Bible tells us not to keep a record of wrongs (1 Corinthians 13:5). Jesus wasn't saying to count up someone's sins. Instead, because all of our sins are forgiven in Jesus, we can forgive those who sin against us.

PARENT Talk Confess to your family if someone (either in your family or outside your family) has hurt you in a way you don't want to forgive. Pray with each other, that God would help everyone in your family forgive others as you have been forgiven in Jesus.

 KNOW IT ★ Showing *mercy and forgiveness* means not treating someone in the way she deserves (Matthew 18:27).

★ You know you have forgiven someone when you no longer hope that he suffers for his sins.

★ We forgive and show mercy because we have been forgiven in Jesus (Ephesians 4:32).

ASK IT

 PRAY IT Ask God to help you show others mercy and forgiveness. Worship Jesus for making a way for your sins to be forgiven.

DAY 6
THE PHARISEE AND THE TAX COLLECTOR

Verse of the Day: Luke 18:9-14

Challenge: Luke 11:1-4

 DO IT Compare the two kinds of prayers. Draw a line from each statement to the kind of person it describes.

I want people to see and hear me

God forgive me

PROUD

I fast twice a week

Thank you I am not like other people

HUMBLE

I give a tenth of everything

 KNOW IT ★ God does not want you to think you are more righteous than other people (Luke 18:9).

★ God does not want you to compare yourself to other people (Luke 18:11-12).

★ God wants you to examine your own life and confess your sin honestly to Him (Luke 18:13).

ASK IT

 PRAY IT Spend some time praying about the parable that impacted you the most this week. Thank Jesus again for speaking in parables and teaching you deeper truths about the kingdom of God.

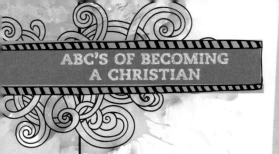

ABC'S OF BECOMING A CHRISTIAN

HOW TO BECOME A CHRISTIAN

Becoming a Christian is the most important decision anyone can ever make. Use the information on this page to tell people about Jesus.

What does the Bible say about becoming a Christian?

★ God loves you (John 3:16).

★ Sin is choosing your way instead of God's way. Sin separates people from God (Romans 3:23).

★ God sent Jesus so you would not have to die for your sin. Jesus died on the cross, He was buried, and God raised Him from the dead (Romans 5:8).

ADMIT

to God you are a sinner (Romans 3:23). Repent, turn away from your sin (Acts 3:19; 1 John 1:9).

BELIEVE

that Jesus is God's Son and receive God's gift of forgiveness from sin (Acts 16:31; Acts 4:12; John 14:6; Ephesians 2:8-9).

CONFESS

your faith in Jesus Christ as Savior and Lord (Romans 10:9-10,13).

The Holy Spirit will help a person know when it is time to become a Christian. If it is not time for your friend to become a Christian, do not push her to do so. God will help her know the right time.

MY STORY

A testimony is a story. When you share your testimony with someone, you are telling him about yourself. Each Christian should be able to tell how she became a Christian. Use these questions to help you write your testimony. Share your testimony with your friends this week.

I first started thinking about becoming a Christian when...

To become a Christian, I needed to...

When I became a Christian, I...

My life is different since I became a Christian in these ways...

I can help someone become a Christian by...

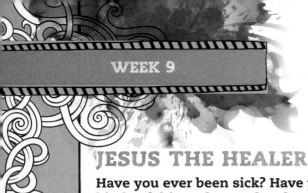

JESUS THE HEALER

Have you ever been sick? Have you ever had to stay in the hospital? What kinds of things do you do when you feel bad? Have you ever tried to comfort someone who was sick?

When Jesus was on earth, He traveled around and healed many sick people. Sickness is a terrible consequence of sin. One reason Jesus healed people was to show that He was the Son of God who had power over sin and all of its effects.

It's important to remember, however, that Jesus does not heal every sick person. In 2 Corinthians 12:7-10, Paul wrote about a "thorn in his flesh." He prayed three times for God to remove whatever was hurting him, but three times God said no. What was Paul's response? "I will most gladly boast all the more about my weaknesses, so that Christ's power may reside in me . . . for when I am weak, then I am strong." Paul understood that sometimes our physical weaknesses, such as illnesses or deformities, can cause us to rely on Jesus even more. Then when other people watch us relying on Jesus, God receives the glory.

God is our great healer. Sometimes He heals quickly and supernaturally. Sometimes He heals us naturally, through doctors or other remedies. Sometimes He chooses to not heal us on earth. But Jesus promises that complete healing is coming in heaven, where there will be no more death, crying, or pain, for all things will be made new (Revelation 21:4-5). For that, we can rejoice!

A second reason Jesus healed people was to show God's love and concern for everyone. Many of the people Jesus healed were considered "unwanted" in Bible times. Lepers, for example, were not allowed to go into the temple or live in the city because of their contagious disease. With just one touch from Jesus, however, they were made clean and could return to normal life again (Matthew 8:1-5). One man possessed with an evil spirit lived in a cave all by himself because no one could properly take care of him. Jesus came along, healed him, and then told him to re-enter his town (Mark 5:1-20). Many religious leaders at the time believed illness was a punishment for sin. But Jesus told them they were wrong and healed a man who had been born blind (John 9:1-12).

Lastly, when Jesus healed people, He did not show favorites. When it came to the rich or the poor, the young or the old, the powerful or the weak, Jesus healed all kinds of people to show that God cares about everyone. All people have access to His great love. Everyone is invited to put their faith in Jesus and find spiritual healing.

"Jesus continued going around to all the towns and villages, teaching in their synagogues, preaching the good news of the kingdom, and healing every disease and every sickness." Matthew 9:35

DAY 1
PETER'S MOTHER—IN—LAW

Verse of the Day: Matthew 8:14-15

Challenge: Mark 1:29-31

DO IT Peter's mother-in-law was sick with a fever. (Peter was one of the disciples.) Jesus touched the woman's hand and she was made well. Think about the last time you were sick with a fever. Draw or make a list of the things you would do if you were home from school because you were sick.

PARENT Talk Spend the entire week praying for someone you know who needs healing.

KNOW IT
★ God cares about things like fevers (Matthew 8:14).
★ Jesus can heal people who are sick with fevers and other ailments (Matthew 8:15).
★ Christians pray for each other when we are sick (James 5:14-16).

ASK IT

PRAY IT If you know someone who is sick, pray for her. Thank God for using His power to heal people. Praise God that when He doesn't heal someone, it is because He has a better plan in mind.

DAY 2
A BLIND MAN

Verse of the Day: John 9:1-12

Challenge: John 9:13-34

DO IT Place a pencil at the starting point, close your eyes, and work the maze. When you think you reached the finish point, open your eyes. How did you do?

Now, keep your eyes open and draw a path through the maze. Was it easier or more difficult to complete the task with your eyes open?

Imagine how the blind man must have felt when he could finally see!

KNOW IT
★ Jesus said the man was not blind because of his sins or the sins of his parents (John 9:3).
★ Jesus touched the man's eyes to heal him (John 9:6).
★ Jesus told the Pharisees that they were *spiritually* blind (John 9:41).

ASK IT

PRAY IT Thank Jesus for teaching that sickness is not a punishment from God. Praise Jesus for being strong enough to heal physical blindness and spiritual blindness. Ask God to open your spiritual eyes so you can see the truth.

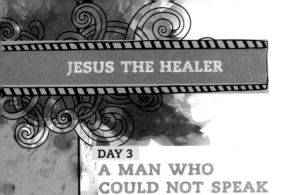
DAY 3
A MAN WHO COULD NOT SPEAK

Verse of the Day: Mark 7:31-37

Challenge: Matthew 9:32-33

 DO IT Jesus healed a man who couldn't speak. Discover a word for someone who cannot speak by figuring out the code. On the blank, place either the letter before or the letter after the one given.

←N →T ←U ←F

What is the longest time you have ever gone without talking? How would your life be different if you were not able to talk?

KNOW IT ★ By touching the man to heal him, Jesus showed him God's love in a special way (Mark 7:33).
★ Soon after Jesus went to heaven, his disciples continued healing people (Acts 3:6).
★ Jesus still heals people today (James 5:15).

 ASK IT

 PRAY IT Thank Jesus for demonstrating God's love through how He healed people. If there is someone you know who needs healing, pray for them right now.

DAY 4
A MAN WHO COULD NOT WALK

Verse of the Day: Mark 2:1-12

Challenge: Mark 2:15-17

 DO IT Imagine playing your favorite sport or outside game. In Box 1, draw the emotion on your face when you are having fun playing. Now imagine you cannot move your legs at all. In Box 2, draw a picture of the emotion on your face when your legs don't work.

1

2

 KNOW IT ★ The man's friends brought him to Jesus. We can bring our sick friends to Jesus by praying for them (Mark 2:4).
★ Jesus forgave the man of his sin (spiritual healing) before He made his legs well (physical healing) (Mark 2:5).
★ God cares most about spiritual healing, or forgiving our sin (Mark 2:9-11).

 ASK IT

 PRAY IT Ask the Holy Spirit to reveal any sin in your life. Ask Him to forgive you for the sin you've committed. Thank God for always forgiving your sins because of what Jesus did on the cross.

DAY 5
TEN MEN WITH A SKIN DISEASE

Verse of the Day: Luke 17:11-19

Challenge: Mark 1:40-45

 DO IT Find the following items around your house. Touch the items and describe how they feel. Are they soft, hard, scratchy, or smooth?

BASKET

COUNTERTOP

DESK

COUCH

Which texture did you like best?
Now touch your skin. Which texture that you felt is closest to your skin's texture?

How do you think the men felt when their skin disease was gone (Luke 17:11-19)?

 PARENT Talk Spend time as a family thanking God for blessings He has given each of you.

 KNOW IT
★ Jesus demonstrated His great power when He healed 10 men with a skin disease (Luke 17:14).
★ Only one man came back and thanked Jesus (Luke 17:15-16).
★ Christians should take time to thank God for His blessings (Psalm 136:1).

ASK IT

 PRAY IT Think of one way God has blessed you recently. Worship God for that, and then tell someone else about it. Continue to praise Jesus for His power to heal, which you are learning about this week.

DAY 6
JAIRUS' DAUGHTER

Verse of the Day: Luke 8:40-42, 49-56

Challenge: John 11:1-43

 DO IT Find these words in the puzzle: heal, Jairus, Jesus, saves, sin.

J	T	E	H	N	S	B	J
X	A	K	M	A	K	Q	E
J	K	I	V	K	J	Z	S
L	A	E	R	P	P	A	U
I	S	U	M	U	W	H	S
K	H	T	D	N	S	U	T
X	L	A	E	H	I	I	O
U	D	S	E	T	B	S	Y

What does each word have to do with the story you read in Luke 8?

Heal: _____

Jairus: _____

Jesus: _____

Saves: _____

Sin: _____

 KNOW IT
★ Jairus had faith that Jesus was strong enough to heal his daughter (Luke 8:41).
★ Jesus was actually strong enough to raise his daughter from the dead (Luke 8:52-54).
★ Jesus promises that one day, every Christian who has died will be raised to life (1 Thessalonians 4:16).

ASK IT

 PRAY IT Worship God for all the healings you read about this week. Tell Jesus which story impacted you the most and why. Keep praying for God to heal anyone you know who is sick.

When you pray, you talk to and listen to God. You can talk to God anywhere and at any time. You don't have to use special words or even close your eyes! You can talk to Him out loud or pray quietly to yourself. God wants you to talk to Him often!

THE WORD PRAY CAN HELP YOU REMEMBER THINGS TO SHARE WITH GOD:

P STANDS FOR PRAISE.
Praise God for who He is and for all He has done for you.

R STANDS FOR REPENT.
When you repent, you tell God what you've done wrong and turn or change from disobeying God to obeying Him.

A STANDS FOR ASK.
God wants you to ask Him for the things other people need.

Y STANDS FOR YOURSELF.
God wants you to pray for yourself too!

Look at the "I Can Pray" hand. Now look at your hand and try to remember what each part of your hand represents. (With your parents' permission, you may want to write the PRAY letters on your fingers to help you remember!)

On the next page, make a prayer list by writing things to include in your prayers using the pray letters.

CHALLENGE:
Memorize the Model Prayer Jesus taught His disciples (Matthew 6:9-13)!

PARENT Talk
This is another page you can share with your parents. After you memorize what the PRAY letters stand for, use your hand to explain to your parents about prayer. Encourage your parents to make a list of things to include in their prayers, then pray with your parents using your lists as a guide.

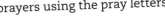

MY PRAYER LIST

P—PRAISE
I CAN PRAISE GOD FOR:

R—REPENT
I NEED TO ASK GOD
TO FORGIVE ME FOR:

A—ASK
I CAN ASK GOD
FOR THESE THINGS OTHER
PEOPLE NEED:

Y—YOURSELF
I CAN ASK GOD FOR THESE
THINGS I NEED:

JESUS THE FRIEND OF SINNERS

If someone asked you why Jesus left heaven and came to earth, what would you say? Before reading any further, close the book and come up with one reason you think Jesus came for you.

There are many answers to this question, and it's impossible to sum them up in one sentence. This is not a full list, but we know for sure that Jesus came to earth because God loves us (John 3:16). He came to be the final sacrifice for sin (John 1:29). He came to destroy the works of the devil (1 John 3:8). He came to fulfill the law and the prophets (Matthew 5:17). He came to preach the truth (John 18:37). He came to give us abundant life (John 10:10). He came to seek and save the lost (Luke 19:10). He came to give sinners a chance to repent of their sins (Luke 5:32).

The religious leaders in Jesus' day did not understand most of these reasons for Jesus' coming. They thought Jesus would be a military ruler who would save Israel from its enemies, making it a strong nation again. They did not realize that the "saving" God had promised in the Old Testament was a *spiritual* saving—a saving of people's hearts through faith.

This is why the religious leaders were confused about how Jesus spent His time. Why wasn't Jesus gathering a bunch of powerful, educated, and holy men together to take down the Romans? Why did He pick greedy tax collectors and uneducated fisherman to be His disciples? Also, if Jesus really came from God, why did He spend lots of time with ungodly people? They expected Jesus to hang out with people who knew the right answers and behaved in the right ways.

Over and over again, Jesus explained that He came to save sinners, people who knew they needed God's mercy. Jesus came for people who recognized God was their only hope. In speaking about one such woman, Jesus said, "Her many sins have been forgiven; that's why she loved much. But the one who is forgiven little, loves little." (Luke 7:47) Jesus was saying that when we realize how badly we need Him, we will love Him (and others) that much more and follow Him even more closely.

So Jesus is not asking you to do all the right things. Jesus is not asking you to know all the right answers. Jesus is asking you to depend on Him for everything, come to Him when you sin, and love Him because of how much He loves you.

Is there something you are trying to hide from Jesus? Is there some sin you have been covering up because you think God will be angry at you for it? Jesus already took all of God's anger for your sin when He died on the cross. You do not need to be afraid to tell Him about it. You don't need to hide. Jesus is the friend of sinners. Jesus loves you so much!

"This is a trustworthy saying, worthy of full acceptance: Christ Jesus came into the world to save sinners." I Timothy 1:15

DAY 1
THE SAMARITAN WOMAN

Verse of the Day: John 4:7-9, 27-29

Challenge: John 4:39-42

 DO IT Complete the image of the clay pot below.

 PARENT Talk Think about the type of people your family spends time with. Do they all look like you? Do they all think like you? Are they all from your country? Brainstorm ways your family could better love people who are different from you. Pick one way and make a plan to do that in the next month.

 **KNOW IT**
★ Jesus (a Jew) spoke to the woman (a Samaritan), even though Jews and Samaritans did not get along (John 4:9).
★ The disciples were surprised Jesus was speaking to a Samaritan woman (John 4:27).
★ Everyone, no matter what their background, can worship God in spirit and truth because of Jesus (John 4:23).

ASK IT

 PRAY IT Ask God to help you see people as He sees them, as equal and in need of His love. If there is someone you often ignore or avoid, ask God for the courage to speak to that person in love.

DAY 2
ZACCHAEUS

Verse of the Day: Luke 19:1-10

Challenge: Matthew 6:19-21

 DO IT Draw a picture of each of your family members. Measure how tall each person is and write the height under the drawing.

Who is the tallest in your family?_____

Who is the shortest in your family?_____

 KNOW IT
★ Zacchaeus' was a tax collector who stole money. People were not happy that Jesus went to his house (Luke 19:7).
★ After Zacchaeus spent time with Jesus, his heart changed (Luke 19:8).
★ Zacchaeus paid the people back even more than he had stolen from them (Luke 19:8).

ASK IT

 PRAY IT Is there someone you believe is too sinful for Jesus to save? Repent of that belief, and start asking God to save that person. Pray about how you might show that person Jesus' love.

JESUS THE FRIEND OF SINNERS

DAY 3
WOMAN WHO ANOINTS JESUS

Verse of the Day: Luke 7:37-39

Challenge: Luke 7:44-48

 DO IT Circle all the things you can give to God or do for Him.

What other things can you give to God? Include not just things you can give, but things you can do.

Why is giving your best to God the right thing to do?

 KNOW IT ★ The woman in today's story gave Jesus an expensive gift (Luke 7:37).
★ She poured her perfume on Jesus to worship Him (Luke 7:38).
★ Jesus explained that the woman loved Him so much because He had forgiven her so much (Luke 7:47).

ASK IT

 PRAY IT Do you ever think about how much Jesus has forgiven you? Praise Him for being a God who forgives all of our sins, no matter how small or how great.

DAY 4
THIEF ON THE CROSS

Verse of the Day: Luke 23:39-43

Challenge: Philippians 1:21-24

 DO IT Trace the large cross, then draw two crosses on either side. These represent the crosses where Jesus and the two thieves were crucified.

 PARENT Talk Pray for someone that your family knows is making bad decisions. Ask God to give that person a chance to repent of her sin. Ask for opportunities to help her and love her as Jesus does.

 KNOW IT ★ Two thieves were crucified next to Jesus (Luke 23:32).
★ One thief mocked Jesus, but the other honored Jesus (Luke 23:41).
★ The thief who honored Jesus trusted in Jesus as his Savior and went to heaven after he died (Luke 23:43).

ASK IT

 PRAY IT Jesus can save anyone, even someone who deserves to be crucified for the terrible things they have done. Praise Jesus for dying on the cross to pay the penalty for all our sins.

DAY 5
THOMAS

Verse of the Day: John 20:24-29

Challenge: 1 Peter 1:8-12

 DO IT Write the opposite of each word. Then put the numbered letters in their correct spaces.

Soft _ _ _ _
1

Cold _ _ _ _
2

Front _ _ _ _ _
4

Open _ _ _ _ _
3 5

_ _ _ _ _ _ _

Doubt is the opposite of faith. Someone who doubts demands to see something *before* they can believe it is possible.

 KNOW IT ★ Thomas doubted that Jesus was alive because he had not seen it for himself (John 20:25).
★ Thomas worshiped Jesus once he saw Him again (John 20:28).
★ Jesus said people who believe in Him *without* seeing Him are blessed (John 20:29).

ASK IT

 PRAY IT Worship Jesus for rising from the dead. Thank Him for blessing anyone who believes in Him without seeing Him. Do you know someone who does not believe in Jesus? Pray for that person.

DAY 6
SAUL, WHO BECAME PAUL

Verse of the Day: Acts 9:1-19

Challenge: 1 Timothy 1:12-14

 DO IT Unscramble the words of the letters that come from today's story.

AULS _ _ _ _

ASCDSUAM

_ _ _ _ _ _ _ _

LAPU _ _ _ _

IHTLG _ _ _ _ _

SSUEJ _ _ _ _ _

INBNL _ _ _ _ _

NNISAAA

_ _ _ _ _ _ _

ZPIABETD

_ _ _ _ _ _ _ _

 KNOW IT ★ Before Saul met Jesus, he persecuted Christians (Acts 9:1, 13).
★ God chose Saul to share the gospel with all kinds of people (Acts 9:15).
★ Saul was a completely different person after meeting Jesus (Acts 9:18).

ASK IT

 PRAY IT Worship Jesus for saving people in crazy ways, like Saul. Thank Him for giving Saul an important job to do. Ask God what job He wants you to do, and pray for the courage to do it.

Saul, Damascus, Paul, light, Jesus, blind, Ananias, baptized

ACROSS

2 Means "Savior"
4 A special story about God's kingdom
5 Means "God with us"
7 The disciple who doubted Jesus
10 Books before Jesus came to earth
11 Means "forever"
13 The Bible is _____ story

DOWN

1 Skills, abilities, belongings, and more
2 When God does something impossible
3 The most important healing
6 Means "to try to get someone to sin"
8 John the _____
9 What is too hard for God
12 Someone you follow and look up to

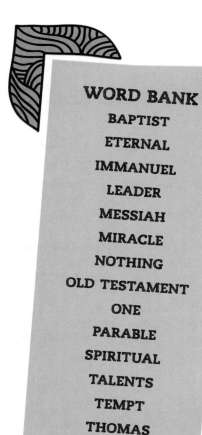

WORD BANK

BAPTIST
ETERNAL
IMMANUEL
LEADER
MESSIAH
MIRACLE
NOTHING
OLD TESTAMENT
ONE
PARABLE
SPIRITUAL
TALENTS
TEMPT
THOMAS

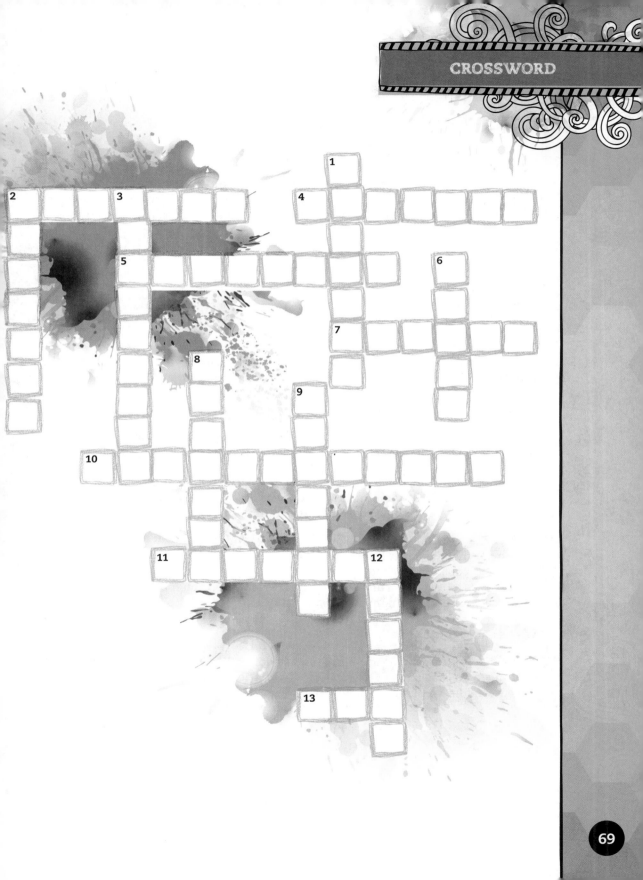

JESUS THE TRUTH TELLER

Have you ever taken a true or false quiz in school? Sometimes it's easy to decide if something is false, but it's not always easy to figure out what the true answer is. For example, can you correct these false phrases to make them all true?

- Kangaroos can live to be 20 feet tall.
- The first airplane took flight in the year 1350.
- The platypus is classified as a bird because it lays eggs.

Did you automatically know all of the ways to make these statements true, or did you have to look them up?

When it comes to the truth, Jesus knows every true answer because He knows all things. But more than that, Jesus is the truth. In John 14:6, He said, "I am the way, the truth, and the life. No one comes to the Father except through me." This means that Jesus cannot lie or deceive. Rather, His words will always be faithful to God. It also means if you want to understand the ways of God, you have to come through Jesus.

You would think that because Jesus never lies or deceives, and because He helps us understand God more, it would always be easy to accept what He says. But sometimes it is hard to listen to Jesus. In the stories you'll read this week, sometimes Jesus' words confused people. Other times they brought comfort. Sometimes they caused people to stop and think about something in a new way. Remember, Jesus always speaks the truth out of love and with our best interests in mind.

When it comes to God's truth, the question will always be, "How will you respond?" Sometimes when you hear Jesus' words, your heart will gladly receive and obey them. Other times, you'll prefer to ignore them. God gave you the ability to choose to follow or reject Jesus, but you will always be most blessed when you follow Him. John 8:31-32 tells us, "If you continue in my word, you really are my disciples. You will know the truth, and the truth will set you free." This is why Jesus tells us the truth: because He loves us and wants us to experience freedom in Him.

So whenever you're reading the Bible and you don't understand the words, the first thing to do is ask God's Holy Spirit for help. Then go ask older, wiser people for their wisdom and understanding too.

"I was born for this, and I have come into the world for this: to testify to the truth. Everyone who is of the truth listens to my voice." John 18:37

True Answers | The largest known kangaroo grew to 6.9 feet. | The Wright Brothers flew their first plane in 1903. | The platypus is classified as a mammal, or specifically a monotreme, because it lays eggs.

DAY 1
NICODEMUS

Verse of the Day: John 3:1-7, 16-17

Challenge: John 3:14-21

 DO IT If you could spend 30 minutes visiting with Jesus, what would you ask Him?

 KNOW IT ★ Even though Nicodemus was a religious leader, He did not understand who Jesus was (John 3:2).

★ To be "born again" means to receive new life from God through Jesus (John 3:16).

★ Anyone who puts their full trust in Jesus is "born again" (John 3:18).

ASK IT

 PRAY IT Thank God for revealing to you the truth about Jesus. Thank Him for offering you new life in Jesus. Pray for friends or family who don't yet know who Jesus is.

 PARENT Talk Ask your parents about the day you were born. How did your parents feel? Discuss how God feels when someone trusts in Jesus (Luke 15:10).

DAY 2
THE RICH YOUNG RULER

Verse of the Day: Matthew 19:16-22

Challenge: Matthew 19:23-26

 DO IT Circle the image you think costs more between the two. Write your estimate of the cost beside each item.

With a parent's help, research the cost of each item online, or go to the store to find out.

 KNOW IT ★ The young man who came to talk to Jesus today was rich.

★ Jesus told him a hard truth: "You must give away your wealth and follow me to receive eternal life" (Matthew 19:21).

★ The man cared too much about his riches and went away sad (Matthew 19:22).

ASK IT

 PRAY IT Is there something so important to you, that you could never give it away? Confess this to God. Tell Him you want to love Him more than anything else.

DAY 3

TWO SISTERS

Verse of the Day: Luke 10:38-42

Challenge: Philippians 4:6-7

DO IT Circle the five differences between the two sisters.

PARENT Talk Consider if your family is distracted by lots of activities or church responsibilities? Brainstorm steps to adjust from any distractions, and choose one step to take this week.

 KNOW IT ★ Mary sat at Jesus' feet and listened to Him talk (Luke 10:39). ★ Martha was distracted by all the work she had to do and complained about her sister Mary (Luke 10:40). ★ Jesus said Mary had made the right choice (Luke 10:42).

ASK IT

 PRAY IT Ask for forgiveness if you have been distracted and not listened to God. If you struggle to spend time with Jesus, pray for help.

DAY 4

THE CHILDREN AND THE DISCIPLES

Verse of the Day: Mark 10:13-16

Challenge: Matthew 18:1-5

 DO IT Fill in the blank with the letter that comes TWO letters after the one provided.

I G L E B M K

M D   E M B

Jesus said this belongs to those who come to God like children.

 KNOW IT ★ The disciples thought Jesus was too important to spend time with children (Mark 10:13). ★ Jesus said in order to enter the kingdom of God, people have to come to God like a child (Mark 10:15). ★ Jesus hugged and blessed the children (Mark 10:16).

ASK IT

 PRAY IT Worship Jesus for loving you and thinking you're important. Thank Him for caring about you and wanting what's best for you. Tell Him anything you're thinking or feeling right now. He wants to hear it.

Answer: Kingdom of God

DAY 5:
THOMAS AND THE DISCIPLES

Verse of the Day: John 14:4-6

Challenge: John 6:41-45

 DO IT Connect the red dots, the blue dots, and the green dots to find out what Jesus calls Himself.

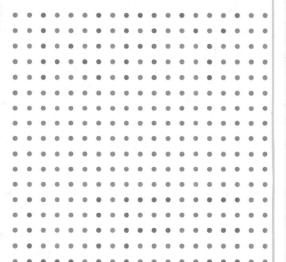

 KNOW IT
★ Jesus said He is the way, the truth, and the life (John 14:6).
★ This means there is no other way to God than through Jesus.
★ This means we cannot find the meaning of life without Jesus.

 ASK IT

 PRAY IT Thank Jesus for making a **way** back to God. Thank Him for the **truth** He reveals in the Bible. Thank Him for the new **life** He gave to you.

DAY 6
PILATE

Verse of the Day: John 18:33-38

Challenge: 1 Timothy 1:15-17

 DO IT Use the given symbols to decode the message.

D	F	G	H	I	K	L	M

N	O	R	S	T	W	Y

 KNOW IT
★ Jesus said His kingdom was not of this world (John 18:36).
★ This was a hard truth for someone like Pilate to understand (John 18:33).
★ Jesus' kingdom is a *spiritual* kingdom.

 ASK IT

 PRAY IT Thank Jesus for being your king. Think about if there is any sin you need to confess to Him. Thank Him for being the best king in all the universe.

73

JESUS FACTS
Check out these facts about Jesus.

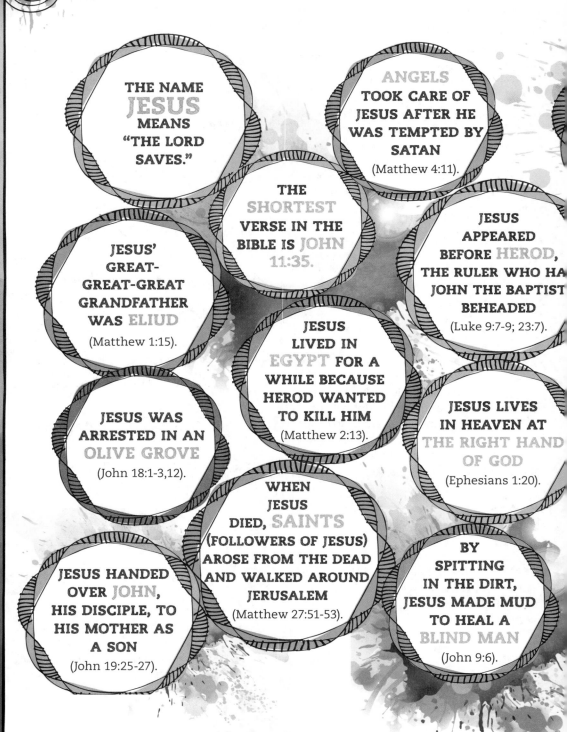

THE NAME **JESUS** MEANS "THE LORD SAVES."

ANGELS TOOK CARE OF JESUS AFTER HE WAS TEMPTED BY SATAN (Matthew 4:11).

THE **SHORTEST** VERSE IN THE BIBLE IS **JOHN 11:35.**

JESUS' GREAT-GREAT-GREAT GRANDFATHER WAS **ELIUD** (Matthew 1:15).

JESUS APPEARED BEFORE **HEROD**, THE RULER WHO HA JOHN THE BAPTIST BEHEADED (Luke 9:7-9; 23:7).

JESUS LIVED IN **EGYPT** FOR A WHILE BECAUSE HEROD WANTED TO KILL HIM (Matthew 2:13).

JESUS WAS ARRESTED IN AN **OLIVE GROVE** (John 18:1-3,12).

JESUS LIVES IN HEAVEN AT **THE RIGHT HAND OF GOD** (Ephesians 1:20).

WHEN JESUS DIED, **SAINTS** (FOLLOWERS OF JESUS) AROSE FROM THE DEAD AND WALKED AROUND JERUSALEM (Matthew 27:51-53).

JESUS HANDED OVER **JOHN**, HIS DISCIPLE, TO HIS MOTHER AS A SON (John 19:25-27).

BY SPITTING IN THE DIRT, JESUS MADE MUD TO HEAL A **BLIND MAN** (John 9:6).

THE NAME **JESUS** APPEARS IN THE BIBLE OVER 900 TIMES.

JESUS IS THE CREATOR OF **EVERYTHING** (Colossians 1:16-17).

ESUS WAS PROBABLY YEARS OLD HEN HE WAS CRUCIFIED.

JESUS IS THE SAME YESTERDAY, TODAY, AND **FOREVER** (Hebrews 13:8).

JESUS WAS NEVER CREATED— HE HAS **ALWAYS EXISTED** (Micah 5:2)

JOHN THE BAPTIST WAS JESUS' RELATIVE.

ALTHOUGH WE CELEBRATE JESUS' BIRTHDAY ON DECEMBER 25, WE DON'T KNOW HIS **ACTUAL BIRTHDAY.**

JESUS HAD **SEVERAL** HALF BROTHERS AND SISTERS (Matthew 12:46-47; 13:55-56).

JESUS WAS PROBABLY ABOUT **30 YEARS OLD** WHEN HE WAS BAPTIZED BY JOHN THE BAPTIST.

WHEN JESUS WAS 12 YEARS OLD, HE SPENT A FEW DAYS IN JERUSALEM **WITHOUT HIS PARENTS** (Luke 2:41-50).

JESUS WAS A **CARPENTER** (Mark 6:3).

JESUS IS **100% GOD** AND **100% HUMAN.**

How many facts did you already know?
How many were new to you?

JESUS THE SERVANT KING

When you hear the word "king," what comes to mind? How about when you hear the word "servant"? Do the servants who live in a palace spend much time with the king? Why or why not?

Jesus can be described as a "servant king." This is an *oxymoron*, or a phrase with two words that contradict each other. Example oxymorons include "jumbo shrimp," "freezer burn," "only choice," and "awfully good." Can you think of another oxymoron?

How is Jesus a *servant king*? Philippians 2 explains it best. Paul, the author of Philippians, first described Jesus as a servant: "Adopt the same attitude as that of Christ Jesus, who, existing in the form of God, did not consider equality with God as something to be exploited. Instead he emptied himself by assuming the form of a servant, taking on the likeness of humanity. And when he had come as a man, he humbled himself by becoming obedient to the point of death—even to death on a cross." (v. 5-8) So Jesus served us in the greatest way possible: by dying for our sins.

Next, Paul wrote about Jesus' kingship: "For this reason God highly exalted him and gave him the name that is above every name, so that at the name of Jesus every knee will bow—in heaven and on earth and under the earth—and every tongue will confess that Jesus Christ is Lord, to the glory of God the Father." (v. 9-11) The word for "Lord" here is another word for ruler or king.

So Jesus came to earth to serve us through His life, death, and resurrection. Then Jesus returned to heaven to reign over everything as king forever. Jesus is our *servant king*.

We also call Jesus a *servant king* because while He was on earth, He did not take a high position or expect to be treated as an earthly king. For example, when Jesus entered Jerusalem, He did not ride in on a regal horse, but on a lowly donkey (Mark 11:1-11). He often withdrew from the crowds of people who adored Him.

Jesus also did not go around demanding fame, power, or riches. Instead, Jesus spent all of His time serving people, especially people no one else wanted to serve. Jesus served by teaching, healing, listening, and providing for people's needs. Through Jesus' service, He revealed the compassionate and tender heart of God.

God says that to be a servant means to not only care about your own life, but about other people's lives (Philippians 2:3-4). It means to seek out ways to meet needs in the world. It means sacrificing what you want so that others will get what they need. Jesus said, "Greater love has no man than this, that He lay down His life for His friends." (John 15:13) To lay down your life is a hard thing to do. But Jesus did not ask you to do something He was unwilling to do. Your servant king Jesus gave up His life on the cross so that you could live with God forever.

"For even the Son of Man did not come to be served, but to serve, and to give his life as a ransom for many." Mark 10:45

DAY 1
NO HOME

Verse of the Day: Luke 9:58

Challenge: Luke 4:16-24

 DO IT In the space below, write or draw five things you would put in your bedroom in your dream home.

 KNOW IT ★ Jesus did not have a place to call his "home" during the three years of His ministry (Luke 9:58).
★ Jesus and His disciples depended on the generosity of other people to live (Luke 8:1-3).
★ Jesus knew the wealth of the world does not satisfy. Jesus did not need a nice house to be happy (Matthew 6:19-20).

ASK IT

 PRAY IT Worship Jesus for living a humble, simple life while He was on earth. Ask Him to give you a heart like His, a heart that trusts in God and not in the wealth of the world.

DAY 2
THE GOOD SHEPHERD

Verse of the Day: John 10:11-14

Challenge: Psalm 23

 DO IT Using the instructions below, practice drawing sheep on a piece of paper.

1. draw a U 2. add ears, eyes, and nostrils 3. add a fluffy cloud

4. add a fluffy body 5. add more wool 6. add legs

 PARENT Talk Ask your parents to tell you a time they remember God being their good shepherd. If you can recall a time God was your good shepherd, share your story too.

 KNOW IT ★ Sheep will wander away into danger if the shepherd does not protect them.
★ We need Jesus to come find us when we wander away from God (Luke 15:3-7).
★ Jesus called Himself the "good shepherd" because He loves us so much, He died for us (John 10:11).

ASK IT

 PRAY IT Thank Jesus for being your good shepherd, for watching over you, protecting you, and dying for you.

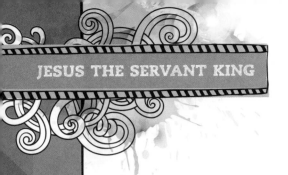
DAY 3
COME TO ME

Verse of the Day: Matthew 11:28-29

Challenge: Philippians 4:4-7

 DO IT Color the yoke on the oxen's backs.

 KNOW IT
★ A *yoke* is wooden cross piece that is secured over two animals' necks and attached to whatever they are pulling.

★ Jesus used the metaphor of the yoke to describe how we should live our lives: walking side by side with Him (Matthew 11:29).

★ Even when life is hard, if we walk with Jesus, we will have peace (Matthew 11:29-30).

ASK IT

 PRAY IT Thank Jesus for walking beside you in life. If something feels like a burden in your life right now, tell Jesus. Ask Him to give you peace as you trust Him.

DAY 4
TO SERVE, NOT BE SERVED

Verse of the Day: Mark 10:45

Challenge: John 15:12-17

 DO IT Write the names of the items. Cross out the letters that are subtracted. Write the letters that remain in the blanks.

Jesus came to _ _ _ _ _ and give His life as a *ransom*.

 PARENT Talk Considering family chores, schedules, and needs, come up with 5-10 ways you can serve each other this month. After brainstorming, every person will pick 1-3 ways he wants to serve the family. Pray together, asking God to give you all servant hearts like Jesus.

 KNOW IT
★ A *ransom* is a payment paid for the release of a prisoner.

★ Jesus said He came to give His life as payment (Mark 10:45).

★ Jesus served us in the greatest way by dying on the cross as payment for our sins (Mark 10:45).

ASK IT

 PRAY IT Praise Jesus for coming to serve and not be served. Thank Him for serving us by dying in our place. Ask God to help you serve others.

DAY 5

KING ON A DONKEY

Verse of the Day: Matthew 21:6-9

Challenge: Matthew 21:1-5

DO IT Play a different version of "pin the tail on the donkey," by closing your eyes and drawing the tail where you think it belongs. Fight the urge to peek!

Zechariah, the Old Testament prophet, said the Messiah would enter Jerusalem on a donkey (Zechariah 9:9).

KNOW IT ★ A donkey was a lowly animal. This represented Jesus' lowly posture of a servant king.
★ The people worshiped Jesus as their Messiah, and He deserved their worship (Matthew 21:9).

ASK IT

PRAY IT Thank Jesus for taking on a lowly position and coming to earth to save us. Ask God to help you not think too highly of yourself, but to have a humble heart like Jesus.

DAY 6:

THE LAST SUPPER

Verse of the Day: Luke 22:19-20

Challenge: Mark 14:12-28

DO IT Inside the pictures, write what Jesus said each one represented.

Flat bread and wine were part of the Passover meal for the Jews. The bread reminded them of how quickly they left slavery in Egypt. They didn't have time to add yeast to their dough! The drink reminded them of the animal sacrifices given for sins.

KNOW IT ★ Jesus said the bread now represented His body, which would be broken for us to set us free (Luke 22:19).
★ Jesus said the drink now represented His blood, which He offered as a final sacrifice for sin (Luke 22:20).
★ Christians still take the Lord's Supper together today to remember what Jesus has done for us.

ASK IT

PRAY IT Praise Jesus for offering His body and blood as a sacrifice for sin. Praise Jesus for being a friend to sinners and a servant king.

79

HOSANNA!

Have you ever seen signs and posters people hold up at sporting events to cheer their teams? That's similar to what the people were doing when they waved palm branches and shouted, "Hosanna!" as Jesus made His way into Jerusalem. The people were praising Jesus and worshiping Him.

Design a sign or poster you could use to praise and worship Jesus.

CRACK THE CODE

Use the code below to decode the words on the page.

2 5 17 22 1 14 1 16 18 6

are commands or rules that . . .
were begun by Jesus.
were taught by the disciples.
were practiced by the early church.
are not required for salvation.

23 18 6 8 6

told us to observe the

2 5 17 22 1 14 1 16 18 6 of

15 14 3 7 22 6 26 and 7 21 18 25 2 5 17 6 ,

6 8 3 3 18 5 with 2 7 21 18 5

16 21 5 22 6 7 22 14 1 6 .

We observe these

2 5 17 22 1 14 1 16 18 6

in our churches today.

Read Matthew 28:18-20 to find out what

23 18 6 8 6

said about

15 14 3 7 22 6 26

Write the verses here:

Read Luke 22:19 to find out what

23 18 6 8 6 said about

7 21 18 25 2 5 17 6   6 8 3 3 18 5 .

Write the verse here:

JESUS BETRAYED AND SENTENCED

Have you ever been *betrayed*? To *betray* someone is to be disloyal to that person. Examples of betrayal include talking about a friend behind her back or breaking a promise. If you have ever been betrayed, how did that feel? If you had known the betrayal was coming, would you have said something to stop it?

Jesus knew Judas was going to betray Him by paying the religious leaders money to arrest Him. Jesus told Judas He knew about his plans, and yet, Jesus did not try to stop him (Matthew 26:21-25). When the guards came to arrest Jesus, He did not fight back. And when Peter cut off one of the guard's ears, Jesus healed the guard and willingly went away to trial.

Jesus is God. He could have easily stopped His betrayal and arrest, but He didn't. Jesus even admitted He had the authority to call thousands of angels to save Him, but instead, He kept the angels at bay (Matthew 26:53). *Why did He do this?*

Jesus had come to earth for a specific job: to live the life we could not live, die the death that we deserved, and come back to life to prove He was God. In fact, long before Jesus was arrested, He told His disciples, "I lay down my life so that I may take it up again. No one takes it from me, but I lay it down on my own" (John 10:17-18).

This is why when Jesus was put on multiple trials, He did not fight back. He did not defend Himself. He did not condemn His accusers. After all, Jesus had submitted Himself to God the Father's plan, and even though it was hard, He did it out of love for God and for us.

It's important to realize that some people thought they had outsmarted Jesus. They said to themselves, "Finally, we've got Him! Finally, Jesus will be punished for His sins!" You see, these people did not hate Jesus because He was good. They hated Him because they thought He was bad. They believed Jesus was committing the worst possible sin by claiming to be the Son of God. (After all, if *you* claimed to be the Son of God, that would be a terrible sin, since *you* are not!) Their spiritual eyes were darkened and they could not see Jesus for who He really was. So in seeking to defend God's honor, they actually condemned God's one and only Son.

Jesus even prayed for these spiritually blind people. He said, "Father forgive them. They don't know what they are doing." (Luke 23:34) Jesus suffered unfairly and unjustly so that even the people who wanted Him dead could find forgiveness through His sacrifice. What incredible love! What amazing grace! What a wonderful Savior we have!

"From then on Jesus began to point out to his disciples that it was necessary for him to go to Jerusalem and suffer many things from the elders, chief priests, and scribes, be killed, and be raised the third day." Matthew 16:21

DAY 1
THIRTY PIECES OF SILVER

Verse of the Day: Matthew 26:14-16

Challenge: Matthew 26:19-25

 DO IT How do you feel when a friend hurts you? Touch your finger on the square that describes how you feel.

How do you think Jesus felt when Judas hurt Him by betraying Him? Touch your finger on the square that describes how you think Jesus felt.

 KNOW IT ★ We can forgive those who hurt us, because God has forgiven us (Ephesians 4:32).
★ Jesus says to forgive anyone who has hurt us for any reason (Mark 11:25).
★ People will let us down sometimes, but God never will (Deuteronomy 31:8).

 ASK IT

 PRAY IT ★ Is there someone you need to forgive? What did they do to hurt you? Ask God to help you forgive them completely, remembering that He has forgiven you for all your sins. Ask God and your parents for guidance on how to love this person in the future.

DAY 2
PRAYER IN THE GARDEN

Verse of the Day: Luke 22:39-43

Challenge: John 6:38-40

 DO IT Unscramble the key words from today's story.

VLSOIE _ _ _ _ _ _

RYAP _ _ _ _

SSEJU _ _ _ _ _

GLNAE _ _ _ _ _

SSPDEIILCE _ _ _ _ _ _ _ _ _

OOBDL _ _ _ _ _

ELEPS _ _ _ _ _

 KNOW IT ★ Jesus prayed three times for God the Father to change His plan (Matthew 26:44).
★ Jesus knew how hard it would be to die for sinners (Luke 22:44).
★ God the Father said no to Jesus' request, and Jesus was strengthened to obey and go to the cross (Matthew 26:45-46).

 ASK IT

PRAY IT Thank Jesus for following through on God's plan so that your sins could be forgiven. Praise Him for modeling how to pray. Ask God for help right now, and conclude your prayer with "Your will be done."

Answers: olives, pray, Jesus, angel, disciples, blood, sleep

83

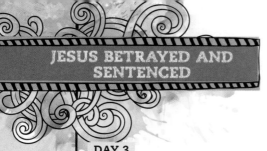

DAY 3
JESUS ARRESTED

Verse of the Day: Matthew 26:47-54

Challenge: Mark 9:30-32

 DO IT Make these scribbles into a picture.

You turned messy squiggles into a clear picture.

 KNOW IT ★ Jesus knew that God would turn His unfair arrest and crucifixion into something beautiful (Hebrews 12:1-2).
★ That beautiful thing is *you!* Because of Jesus, you are saved and being transformed to be more like Him (Romans 8:29).
★ You can trust that God is making beautiful things out of your hard situations (Romans 8:28).

ASK IT

 PRAY IT Thank Jesus for setting the example of trusting God even in hard circumstances. Is there something that is hard for you to trust God with right now? Pray for even more faith and trust.

DAY 4
JESUS AND THE HIGH PRIEST

Verse of the Day: Mark 14:60-64

Challenge: 1 Peter 2:21-23

 DO IT Unscramble the following word.

DEUQOCERN

- - - - - - - - - -

HINT: You can find the word used in John 16:33 in some Bible translations. The word means "overcame."

After you figure the word out, see how many other words you can make by rearranging the letters. The words in your list must have at least three letters each. Don't give up until you've come up with at least five new words!

 KNOW IT ★ The high priest did not believe Jesus was the Son of God. He thought Jesus was *blaspheming*, or disrespecting God (Mark 14:64).
★ Jesus said He would conquer sin and death and one day return to earth on the clouds (Mark 14:62).
★ Jesus set an example in how to suffer through unjust treatment (1 Peter 2:21-23).

ASK IT

 PRAY IT Thank Jesus for the example He set when He was on trial before the high priest. Jesus did not threaten or say mean things. When people treat you poorly, ask God for a heart like Jesus.

DAY 5
THREE ROOSTER CROWS

Verse of the Day: Matthew 26:33-34, 69-75

Challenge: John 21:15-19

DO IT Color by number:
1-red, 2-orange, 3-black

PARENT Talk Ask your parents if they have ever denied knowing, loving, or following Jesus. If you can remember a time you did the same, confess that too. Pray for boldness for your family in sharing the gospel.

KNOW IT ★ Peter said he would never deny Jesus, but Jesus said a rooster would crow after Peter denied Him three times (Matthew 26:34-35).
★ Peter was sorry for denying Jesus (Matthew 26:73-75).
★ Jesus forgave Peter. He gave Peter a job to take care of His sheep, or followers (John 21:15-17).

ASK IT

PRAY IT Pray: Worship Jesus for knowing the sins he will commit in the future and loving us anyway. Thank Jesus for forgiving us for our repeated sins just as He forgave Peter.

DAY 6
BARABBAS RELEASED, JESUS CONDEMNED

Verse of the Day: Matthew 27:15-23

Challenge: Acts 3:12-19

DO IT Draw lines from the statements to the correct person: Jesus or Barabbas.

A murderer (Mark 15:7)
A teacher and healer
A righteous man

A guilty man
Released
Crucified

JESUS

BARABBAS

KNOW IT ★ Pilate did not want to crucify Jesus, because he knew Jesus had done nothing wrong (Matthew 27:24).
★ The Jewish people insisted that Jesus be crucified, so Pilate agreed. Pilate said they were responsible (Matthew 27:25-26).
★ Peter gave the Jews a chance to repent of the sin of crucifying Jesus (Acts 3:12-19).

ASK IT

PRAY IT Praise God that even when we sin in the most terrible of ways, God offers us forgiveness through Jesus. Ask God to give you strength like Jesus when you are treated unfairly.

85

PEOPLE MATCH

Review the Bible stories you read this week. Draw lines from the clues to the correct person. For extra fun, ask someone to call these out to you and see how fast you can say which person it was.

PETER JUDAS PILATE JESUS

Said "I will never run away!"

His wife told him to have nothing to do with Jesus.

Betrayed Jesus with a kiss

Was willing to suffer because of His great love for you and me

Told Peter, "Tonight before the rooster crows you will deny Me three times."

He said, "I am innocent of this man's blood."

Tried to protect Jesus with a sword

Took 30 pieces of silver from those wanting to hurt Jesus

He condemned Jesus to crucifixion.

CHALLENGE CLUE

★ Was a disciple of Jesus: _____

★ Did not think Jesus was guilty: _____

★ Ate together at the Last Supper: _____

JESUS' TRIAL

Search Matthew 26:57—27:31 and write the verses where you read about the people. The first one is done for you.

Jesus: Matthew 26:57,62-64; Matthew 27:1-2,11-14,26-31

Caiaphas: _____

Peter: _____

Sanhedrin: _____

Pilate: _____

Judas: _____

Barabbas: _____

Crowd: _____

Soldiers: _____

Find the names listed above in the puzzle.

E	O	H	S	S	V	B	V	N	H	I	C
T	K	U	A	P	R	S	J	G	D	A	L
A	C	E	N	E	U	E	Z	U	I	N	N
L	R	Q	H	S	H	P	I	A	D	L	N
I	O	P	E	T	E	R	P	D	O	A	C
P	W	J	D	G	L	H	D	V	L	B	S
H	D	G	R	U	A	N	F	N	A	O	Z
U	J	B	I	S	J	H	X	J	Y	N	S
A	C	S	N	S	A	B	B	A	R	A	B

JESUS' DEATH AND RESURRECTION

Remember many weeks ago when you learned about Jesus in the Old Testament? All the way back in the beginning of the Bible, God said He would send someone to destroy evil. God told Satan, "He will strike your head, and you will strike his heel" (Genesis 3:15). In other words, Jesus would conquer Satan, but Satan would hurt Jesus. In Isaiah 53, Isaiah also prophesied that Jesus would be pierced and crushed because of sin. God promised to heal us because of Jesus' wounds.

So Jesus knew what was coming, and that His time for great suffering had arrived. After Pilate condemned Jesus to death, the guards whipped Him, spat on Him, mocked Him, and nailed Him to a cross. Even though Jesus is God, He was also completely human. His whole body suffered tremendously. Despite the pain, Jesus stayed there, on the cross, to be your *substitute sacrifice*. A *substitute* is someone who takes your place. A *sacrifice* is when someone gives something up for you. Jesus is your *substitute sacrifice* because He gave up His life to take the punishment for your sin.

Right before Jesus died, He said, "It is finished." These three words are very important to Christians, because they mean that no one will ever die for sin again. Hebrews 10:10 says, "We have been sanctified through the offering of the body of Jesus Christ once for all time." This means that Jesus' substitute sacrifice was perfectly enough. Once and for all time, you are forgiven in Jesus.

Right after Jesus died, most people thought that was the end. Even though Jesus had told them He would rise three days later, nobody understood Him (Luke 24:7). After all, dead people don't just come back to life! But this is what God meant in Genesis 3:15 when He told Satan, "He will strike your head." Jesus' resurrection was a "death blow" to Satan. His resurrection showed that Jesus is stronger than every evil force. Death could not keep Jesus down. Satan is limited in his power, but Jesus is unlimited. And His power will last forever.

After Jesus rose again, He appeared to His disciples and over 500 witnesses to prove that He really was alive. The question now was, *What would the disciples do about it? Would they keep the good news of Jesus to themselves, or would they go out and tell the world?*

This is the same question for Christians today. Now that we have this news that Jesus died and rose again, do we keep it to ourselves? Not at all. We share what we believe with those who don't know Jesus so that they can put their faith in His substitute sacrifice too.

"He is not here. For he has risen, just as he said. Come and see the place where he lay." Matthew 28:6

DAY 1
JESUS WAS MOCKED

Verse of the Day: Matthew 27:27-31

Challenge: Matthew 27:32-44

 DO IT Circle all the expressions that show how you feel if someone makes fun of you.

What hurts the most about being made fun of?

 PARENT Talk Invite everyone in the family to remember a time he finished a big project. Ask, "How did it feel to be finished?" Together, worship Jesus for staying on the cross to pay the full penalty for sin, so He could say, "It is finished."

 KNOW IT ★ Jesus was made fun of for claiming to be God's Son. (Matthew 27:42-43).
★ One day everyone will know the truth, and all will bow before Jesus as Lord (Philippians 2:9-10).
★ Jesus understands how it feels to be mocked. He can help you love the people who make fun of you (Hebrews 4:15).

ASK IT

 PRAY IT Worship Jesus for suffering for you. Praise Him for not hating the people who mocked Him. Ask Him to help you love those who make fun of you.

DAY 2
JESUS WAS CRUCIFIED

Verse of the Day: Luke 23:33-34

Challenge: Mark 15:33-41

 DO IT Draw three small dots on the cross, two on the left and the right sides, and one at the bottom. These dots represent the nails that went through Jesus' hands and feet. Draw a big heart around the cross, and remember that Jesus stayed on the cross because God loves you.

 KNOW IT ★ Jesus stayed on the cross for about 6 hours (Mark 15:25, 34).
★ For three hours, darkness covered the land, and Jesus suffered greatly (Mark 15:33).
★ People who loved Jesus came to watch Him die (John 19:25-27).

ASK IT

 PRAY IT Tell Jesus how this story makes you feel. Praise Jesus for understanding you whenever you are sad and hurting. Thank Him for staying on the cross to pay for your sins.

89

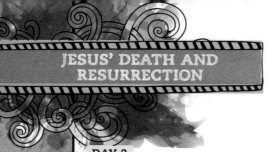

DAY 4
JESUS WAS BURIED

Verse of the Day: Matthew 27:57-61

Challenge: Matthew 27:62-66

 DO IT Using a crayon or marker, color the entire box below black. Leave no white space at all.

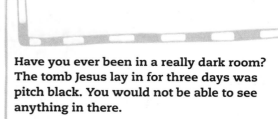

Have you ever been in a really dark room? The tomb Jesus lay in for three days was pitch black. You would not be able to see anything in there.

 KNOW IT
★ Jesus was buried in one of His disciple's tombs (Matthew 27:57).
★ A heavy stone was rolled in front of the tomb, so it was impossible to get in or out (Matthew 27:60).
★ The Pharisees placed guards at the tomb, just in case His disciples tried to steal His body (Matthew 27:64-66).

ASK IT

 PRAY IT Do you ever think you can outsmart God, like the Pharisees did with setting a guard at the tomb? Confess those thoughts to God. Admit that you cannot outsmart Him, and tell Him you want to trust Him more.

DAY 3
IT IS FINISHED

Verse of the Day: John 19:28-30

Challenge: Romans 6:9-10

 DO IT How do you know when you are finished? Draw a line from the word on the left to the phrase on the right

a test	final credits
a race	finish line
a book	empty wrapper
a movie	"Time's up!"
a candy bar	last sentence

When Jesus was finished paying the penalty for sin, He said, "It is finished" and gave up His spirit.

 KNOW IT
★ When Jesus died, the curtain in the temple was torn in two. This showed that because of Jesus' sacrifice, you can freely enter God's presence (Mark 15:38).
★ When Jesus died, one of the soldiers said, "Surely, this was the Son of God!" (Mark 15:39).
★ Nobody will ever need to die for sin again (Romans 6:10).

 ASK IT

 PRAY IT Worship Jesus for finishing the work God the Father gave Him to do. Thank Him for making a way for all people to enter God's presence. Tell Jesus that, like the soldier, you believe He is the Son of God.

DAY 5
JESUS IS ALIVE!

Verse of the Day: Matthew 28:1-6

Challenge: Matthew 28:7-15

 DO IT Jesus is no longer dead. He is alive! Can you remember the things the women saw when they went to the tomb?

Use the letters in the box to fill in the blanks. Cross out the letters as you use them.

A I P   E O G E   L B I E
R E L D S   G L W D O I T   R I R
E   L   S   O   W E   G Y E T A

★ An __N_E_ of the L_R__

★ The __T_N_ was __O_L_D back

★ The angel's appearance was like _I_H_N_N_ and his __O_E as __H_T_ as __N_W

★ The tomb was __M_T__. Jesus was not __H_R__. He had been __A_S_D from the __E_D.

 PARENT Talk Talk about funerals and everyone's experience with them. Why are funerals so sad? Why do we need to tell people *both* about Jesus' death *and* resurrection?

 KNOW IT ★ Three days after He died, Jesus rose from the dead and is alive (Matthew 28:1, 5-6).
★ The same power that raised Jesus from the dead lives in all Christians (Romans 8:11).

 ASK IT

 PRAY IT Praise Jesus for being alive today! Tell Him you believe that the same power that raised Him from the dead lives in you.

DAY 6
JESUS APPEARED TO HIS DISCIPLES

Verse of the Day: Luke 24:36-43

Challenge: 1 Corinthians 15:3-8

 DO IT Do the math. A lot of people saw Jesus alive after He was resurrected. Look up each verse and write in the blank the number of people who saw Jesus.

_____ LUKE 24:13—15

_____ LUKE 24:33—43

_____ JOHN 20:11—16

_____ 1 CORINTHIANS 15:6

_____ 1 CORINTHIANS 15:8

 KNOW IT ★ Jesus appeared first to two women after He rose from the dead (Matthew 28:5-8-9).
★ Jesus did not return to heaven right after He rose from the dead (1 Corinthians 15:5-8).
★ Instead, Jesus appeared to over 500 people, including all of His disciples (1 Corinthians 15:5-8).

 ASK IT

 PRAY IT Thank Jesus for staying on earth to minister to people before He went back to heaven. Spend time reviewing the stories from this week and worship Jesus for what you recall.

Instructions:
Locate a **game piece** for each player, and a **coin**. Place game pieces on the "Start" space. Take turns flipping the coin to determine how many spaces to move:
Heads ☆ 1 space   Tails ☆ 2 spaces

18. Jesus was raised from the dead (Easter)!
Move forward 2 spaces.

Finish
Celebrate that Jesus is alive!

17. Jesus was buried in a sealed, guarded tomb.

16. Jesus died.

15. Jesus was crucified between two criminals (Good Friday).

14. Soldiers mocked Jesus.

13. Crowds shouted, "Crucify Him!"
Go back 3 spaces.

12. Jesus was put on trial.

11. Jesus was arrested.

10. Judas betrayed Jesus with a kiss.
Go back 1 space.

NOTE: You can help the game board lay more flat by laying heavier objects (like books) on the outside edges of your journal. Use coins, different colored paper clips or squares of paper, or other small objects for game pieces.

Read the event on each space as you land on it. Find the verses in Matthew 21:1–28:10 that match the space. Follow any directions on the space to move forward or backward before the next player makes his move. The first person to reach the "Finish" space will shout, "Jesus is alive!"

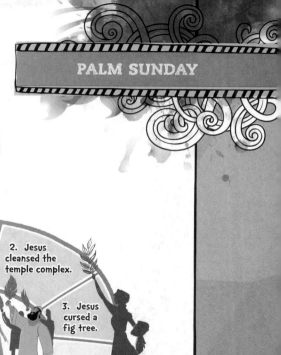

Start

1. People praised Jesus as He entered Jerusalem (Palm Sunday). Move forward 2 spaces.

2. Jesus cleansed the temple complex.

3. Jesus cursed a fig tree.

4. Children praised Jesus. Move forward 1 space.

5. Jesus told parables and made predictions.

6. A plot was made to kill Jesus. Move back 2 spaces.

7. Jesus was anointed at Bethany. Move forward 1 space.

8. Jesus celebrated the Passover with His disciples.

9. Jesus prayed in the garden of Gethsemane.

PARENT Talk Invite your parents to play this game with you. As you move your game pieces around the board, work together to find the verses in Matthew 21:1–28:10 that match the spaces. Who will reach the finish space first?

JESUS THE KING OF KINGS

Do you know that a lot of the Bible is about waiting? Abraham waited about 25 years for God to give his wife a son. David waited 20 years after his anointing to become king. The Jews waited 400 years to be freed from Egypt, then 40 more years to enter the promised land. Even Jesus waited 30 years before He started His ministry on earth.

Waiting is hard. God knows that. It's hard to wait in line. It's hard to wait for dinner. It's hard to wait for your birthday to arrive. More than that, for Christians, it's really hard to wait for Jesus to return. Jesus promised in the Book of Revelation that when He comes again, He will get rid of Satan once and for all. After He does this, everyone who trusts in Jesus will live forever with God. All things will be new and there will be no more death, crying or pain (Revelation 21:1-5). Jesus said nobody knows when this will happen, so it's our job to wait in faith.

God gives us instructions for how to wait in faith throughout the Bible:

"Wait for the Lord; be strong, and let your heart be courageous." Psalm 27:14

"I wait for the Lord; I wait and put my hope in his word." Psalm 130:5

"Don't say, 'I will avenge this evil!' Wait on the Lord, and he will rescue you." Proverbs 20:22

"It is clear what sort of people you should be in holy conduct and godliness as you wait for the day of God and hasten its coming." 2 Peter 3:11-12

So while we wait, we obey God and hope in His word. We obey because, even though we can't see Jesus, we trust what the Bible says: Jesus is alive today, ruling over the universe as King of kings. Obeying Jesus' words is one way to show people that, even though they can't see Jesus, He is real and He is in charge. While we wait for Jesus to come back, we also have a chance to tell people they can be saved because Jesus died for them.

In fact, Jesus promised He would not return until all people have had a chance to hear this good news (Matthew 24:14). After all, God promises that there will be people from every nation, tribe, people, and language worshiping Him in heaven (Revelation 7:9). This is one of the reasons Jesus has not yet come back—because there are still people around the world who need to hear about Him.

Think about how you want to live your life as you wait for Jesus' return. Do you want to live for yourself, or do you want to live for Him? How do you hope to do that? Who will help you do that?

"Look, I am coming soon! Blessed is the one who keeps the words of the prophecy of this book." Revelation 22:7

DAY 1
THE GREAT COMMISSION

Verse of the Day: Matthew 28:16-20

Challenge: Acts 1:7-11

 DO IT When Jesus ascended, the disciples stood gazing into heaven. What did the angels tell the disciples? Write the conversation in the bubbles.

 KNOW IT ★ We can share the gospel freely, because Jesus has all authority in heaven and on earth (Matthew 28:18-20).
★ People cannot believe in Jesus if they have not heard about Him (Romans 10:14).
★ It is beautiful when we take the good news to those who have never heard it (Romans 10:15).

ASK IT

 PRAY IT Praise Jesus for having all authority in heaven and on earth. Tell Him you want to share His good news with others. Ask Him for courage and help doing that.

DAY 2
PREPARING A PLACE FOR US

Verse of the Day: John 14:1-3

Challenge: Revelation 7:9-12

 DO IT Imagine someone special to you is visiting from out of town. Write down everything your family would do to prepare for their arrival. Work with your parents or siblings to fill out the list.

☐ _____   ☐ _____
☐ _____   ☐ _____
☐ _____   ☐ _____
☐ _____   ☐ _____
☐ _____   ☐ _____

 KNOW IT ★ Jesus said He is preparing a place for every Christian (John 14:2-3).
★ We do not know what these rooms will look like. But we know they will be perfect, because God is perfect (Revelation 21:2-4).
★ Jesus said because He is preparing a place for you, He will come back and you will be with Him forever (John 14:3).

ASK IT

 PRAY IT Thank Jesus for working to prepare a place for you. Praise Him for coming back for you one day. Tell Him you believe your future with Him is real.

DAY 3
PRAYING FOR US

Verse of the Day: Romans 8:34

Challenge: Hebrews 7:25

 DO IT Use the chart to decode the word.

1 A	6 F	11 K	16 P	21 U
2 B	7 G	12 L	17 Q	22 V
3 C	8 H	13 M	18 R	23 W
4 D	9 I	14 N	19 S	24 X
5 E	10 J	15 O	20 T	25 Y
				26 Z

___ ___ ___ ___ ___ ___ ___ ___ ___
9 14 20 5 18 3 5 4 5

To *intercede* means to speak up on someone else's behalf. It means to advocate for someone.

 KNOW IT ★ Jesus *intercedes* for you, or prays for you, before God the Father (Romans 8:34).
★ The Bible says Jesus is alive and interceding for us today (Hebrews 7:25).

ASK IT

 PRAY IT Praise Jesus for being alive today and reigning in heaven with God the Father. Thank Him for talking to God the Father about you. Tell Him how this makes you feel.

DAY 4
RULING OVER THE EARTH

Verse of the Day: Revelation 1:5

Challenge: Colossians 2:9-10

DO IT Write the names of the continents inside their outlines.

NORTH AMERICA SOUTH AMERICA
ASIA EUROPE AFRICA AUSTRALIA

The world has seven continents and six oceans. The distance around the earth at the equator is about 25,000 miles. Currently, about 7.6 billion people live on the earth.

 KNOW IT ★ Jesus reigns over all the kings, presidents, and rulers of the earth (Revelation 1:5).
Jesus is King of kings and Lord of lords (Revelation 19:16).
★ The Bible tells us to pray for our earthly leaders (1 Timothy 2:1-2).

ASK IT

 PRAY IT Praise Jesus for being more powerful than every other ruler. Tell Him you trust His decisions as King. Pray for the leader of your country, that God would give that person wisdom.

DAY 5
RETURNING ONE DAY

Verse of the Day: Mark 13:32

Challenge: Matthew 24:42-44

 DO IT Write one thing you would do after the action described.

You cut your hand. You

You finish eating dinner. You •

You graduate kindergarten. You

You open your birthday presents. You •

You receive your allowance. You •

Jesus promised that sometime *after* the gospel has been shared around the world, He will come back (Matthew 24:14).

 PARENT Talk As a family, commit to minister to one person, or a whole family, at your school, work, or neighborhood this month. Seek opportunities to share the gospel with that person, or family, as you serve and love them well.

 KNOW IT ★ No one knows the exact day when Jesus will return (Mark 13:32-33).
★ When Jesus returns, He will bring everyone who has trusted in Him to be with Him forever (1 Thessalonians 4:16-17).

ASK IT

 PRAY IT Tell Jesus you trust that He will come back at the perfect time. Ask Him for faith and courage to share the good news with as many people as you can.

DAY 6
MAKING ALL THINGS NEW

Verse of the Day: Revelation 21:5

Challenge: Revelation 21:1-4, 22-27

 DO IT Circle the brand new items. Put a square around the worn-out items.

 KNOW IT ★ When you belong to God, you are a new creation. God cleanses you of sin and makes you white as snow (2 Corinthians 5:17, Isaiah 1:18).
★ Jesus is restoring the whole world. One day, He will make everything new and right again (Revelation 21:1-5).
★ In the new heaven and new earth, all Christians will worship God and live in perfect love forever (Revelation 7:9, Revelation 21:22-27).

ASK IT

 PRAY IT Praise Jesus for making you a new creation and cleansing you of your sin. Worship Him for being big enough and powerful enough to restore the world.

JESUS' NAMES ACTIVITY

Fill in the chart, either with the missing name or meaning. You can use the Bible reference to help you figure out the answer. Ask parents for help if you get stuck.

NAME	MEANING	BIBLE REFERENCE
Immanuel		Matthew 1:23
	Brings the kingdom of God	Matthew 9:27
Christ, or Messiah		Matthew 16:16, John 4:25
	Divine title of suffering and exaltation	Matthew 20:28
Word	Reveals God	John 1:1
	Life sacrificed for sin	John 1:29, Revelation 5:12
Savior		John 4:42
	Gives guidance and protection	Psalm 23, John 10:10-11
	Jesus' unique relationship with God the Father	John 20:31
Alpha and Omega		Revelation 21:6
Lord	Sovereign Creator and Redeemer	Romans 10:9

God with us, Son of David, Chosen One of God, Son of Man, Lamb of God, Delivers from sin, Good Shepherd, Son of God, The Beginning and the End

Discuss these names of Jesus with your parents. Talk about different situations in life where remembering a specific name would help you.

Write your favorite name of Jesus in large letters in the box and decorate it.

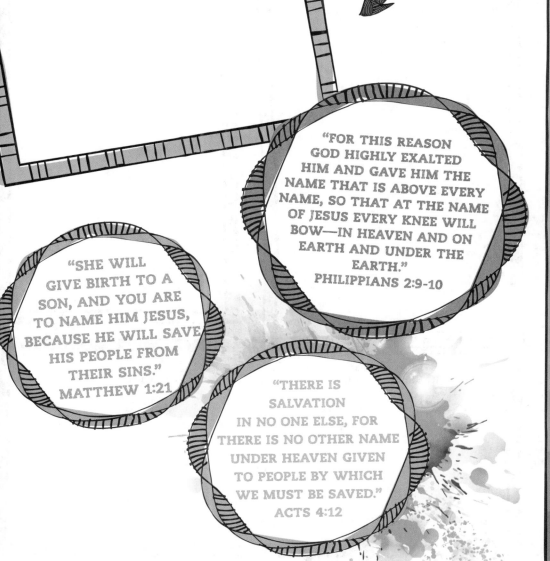

"FOR THIS REASON GOD HIGHLY EXALTED HIM AND GAVE HIM THE NAME THAT IS ABOVE EVERY NAME, SO THAT AT THE NAME OF JESUS EVERY KNEE WILL BOW—IN HEAVEN AND ON EARTH AND UNDER THE EARTH."
PHILIPPIANS 2:9-10

"SHE WILL GIVE BIRTH TO A SON, AND YOU ARE TO NAME HIM JESUS, BECAUSE HE WILL SAVE HIS PEOPLE FROM THEIR SINS."
MATTHEW 1:21

"THERE IS SALVATION IN NO ONE ELSE, FOR THERE IS NO OTHER NAME UNDER HEAVEN GIVEN TO PEOPLE BY WHICH WE MUST BE SAVED."
ACTS 4:12

OVER THE LAST 15 WEEKS YOU'VE LEARNED A LOT ABOUT THE LIFE OF JESUS!

Look back through your journal to help you respond to the questions in the boxes below.

What are three things you learned about Jesus you didn't already know?

1.

2.

3.

What was your favorite topic to study about Jesus?

Why?

If a friend asked you to describe Jesus' life, what would you tell her?

Jesus...

What questions do you still have about Jesus?

ASK YOUR PARENTS,
A TEACHER,
OR A FRIEND
TO HELP YOU
DISCOVER THE
ANSWERS TO
YOUR QUESTIONS.

What will you do to be a better follower of Jesus?

I will ...

Complete this prayer:

Dear Heavenly Father,
Thank You for sending
Jesus ...

In Jesus' name I pray, Amen.

"I am the Alpha and the Omega, the first and the last, the beginning and the end."

Revelation 22:13

"For a child will be born for us, a son will be given to us, and the government will be on his shoulders. He will be named Wonderful Counselor, Mighty God, Eternal Father, Prince of Peace."

Isaiah 9:6

"And a voice from heaven said: 'This is my beloved Son, with whom I am well-pleased.'"

Matthew 3:17

"Love the Lord your God with all your heart, with all your soul, and with all your mind. This is the greatest and most important command. The second is like it: Love your neighbor as yourself."

Matthew 22:37-39

"And Jesus increased in wisdom and stature, and in favor with God and with people."

Luke 2:52

"For you were called to this, because Christ also suffered for you, leaving you an example, that you should follow in his steps."

1 Peter 2:21

"These are written so that you may believe that Jesus is the Messiah, the Son of God, and that by believing you may have life in his name."

John 20:31

"From then on Jesus began to point out to his disciples that it was necessary for him to go to Jerusalem and suffer many things from the elders, chief priests, and scribes, be killed, and be raised the third day."

Matthew 16:21

"I was born for this, and I have come into the world for this: to testify to the truth. Everyone who is of the truth listens to my voice."

John 18:37

"For even the Son of Man did not come to be served, but to serve, and to give his life as a ransom for many."

Mark 10:45

"Jesus continued going around to all the towns and villages, teaching in their synagogues, preaching the good news of the kingdom, and healing every disease and every sickness."

Matthew 9:35

"Jesus told the crowds all these things in parables. . .so that what was spoken through the prophet might be fulfilled."

Matthew 13:34-35

"He is not here. For he has risen, just as he said. Come and see the place where he lay."

Matthew 28:6

"Look, I am coming soon! Blessed is the one who keeps the words of the prophecy of this book."

Revelation 22:7

WORSHIP NOTES

WHO IS TEACHING?

BOOK: _____

CHAPTER: _____

VERSE: _____

Things my pastor/teacher said:

Something I learned about God today:

Something I can do this week related to what I learned or heard in worship:

Something I can talk with my family about related to what I learned or heard in worship:

WHO IS TEACHING?

BOOK: _____

CHAPTER: _____

VERSE: _____

things my pastor/teacher said:

Something I learned about God today:

Something I can do this week Related to what I learned or heard in worship:

Something I can talk with my family about Related to what I learned or heard in worship:

FIRST THINGS FIRST: WHAT IS THE GOSPEL?

The gospel is the good news that God sent His Son Jesus to die for sinners. God made us and loves us, but we have a problem. We sin. We do not want what God wants, and our sin keeps us from knowing God. Jesus came to earth to pay the penalty for our sin. All who trust in Jesus are freely and fully forgiven of their sin and will live with God forever.

WHO SAVES PEOPLE?

God saves people. As you share the gospel, it is not your job to convince people that you are right about Jesus. Instead, share the good news out of love for God and love for people. Pray that whoever you are talking to would hear the truth and believe.

STARTING POINTS

You can share the gospel from many starting points.

GOD, OUR CREATOR

Ask the person to consider what God has made: the oceans, the mountains, the stars, and more. Talk about how God, who made everything, loves us and wants a relationship with us. However, we cannot have a relationship with Him because of our sin. That's why Jesus came. Explain the rest of the gospel message. Ask, "Do you believe this too?"

HUMANITY

Ask your friend to consider how humans are unique, or special. Talk about how we are so special that God wants to have a relationship with us. However, we cannot have a relationship with Him because of our sin. That's why Jesus came. Explain the rest of the gospel message. Ask, "Do you believe this too?"

JESUS

Ask your friend if she has ever heard of Jesus. What does she know about Him? What does she think about Him? Tell her why Jesus came to earth and explain the rest of the gospel message. Ask, "Do you believe this too?"

YOURSELF

Tell your friend how you became a Christian. Tell him what you believe is true about Jesus, and explain the gospel message. Tell him what is different about your life because you follow Jesus. Ask, "Do you believe this too?"

EXAMPLES FROM THE BIBLE

Read the following stories of Jesus' disciples sharing the good news with others. Choose one story and consider the Who, When, What, How, and Why of it. (Refer to Family Discussion Guide.)

★ Peter and the Jews (Acts 2:22-41)
★ Philip and the Ethiopian (Acts 8:26-40)
★ Paul and Barnabas (Acts 14:8-22)
★ Paul in Athens (Acts 17:16-34)
★ Paul before the king (Acts 26:12-29)

DON'T FORGET TO PRAY

Before, during, and after sharing the gospel, it's important to pray. Below is a list of things you can pray for. Can you think of any others?

★ People to share with
★ Opportunities to share
★ Courage and boldness to share
★ Grace and love when sharing
★ The right words when sharing
★ For God to save people

Remember that everyone who hears the good news does not become a Christian right away. That's OK! God saves people according to His perfect plan. You can simply keep praying, loving, and telling others about Jesus.

TIME TO PRACTICE

Practice sharing the gospel with a parent or family member. Remember what you learned in "First Things First" and try to use one of the "Starting Points."

Congratulations! You completed your Life of Jesus journal. So now what?

On pages 100-101 you wrote things you learned about Jesus as you read the Bible and completed the activities. God wants you to continue learning about Jesus, following Him, and telling other people about Him! Here are some ways you can do that:

☆ Attend Bible study classes at your church.

☆ Participate in worship services.

☆ Read and study your Bible each day.

☆ Pray.

☆ Memorize Bible verses.

☆ Tell your family and friends what you know about Jesus.

☆ Ask questions when you do not understand things.

☆ Talk with people who you know have a close relationship with Jesus.

☆ Read stories about people's relationships with Jesus.

☆ Be open to God doing amazing things in your life.

Can you add some other ways to the list?

DEAR PARENTS,

Your child has completed the *Life of Jesus* journal. Celebrate your child's accomplishment! Tell your child some of your favorite moments from Parent Talks, when they came to you with a question, or during family discussion time. Remember that although your child's work on this journal is complete, her journey as a follower of Jesus continues! Here are some suggestions to help your child continue to grow closer to Jesus:

☆ Ask the Holy Spirit to grow your child's desire to read the Bible, pray, and obey.

☆ As a family, participate in a local church through worship and service.

☆ Take the light of Christ into your neighborhood, community, and world.

☆ Model Christlikeness and spiritual disciplines for your child.

☆ Accept your God-given responsibility to train and nurture your child in the ways of the Lord.

☆ Provide additional resources for your child to grow in his spiritual life.

EVEN MORE STORIES

Here are 10 stories from the life of Jesus that were not covered in this devotional. Invite your kids to read these on their own, or use them as an opportunity for family devotions:

☆ Salt and Light (*Matthew 5:13-16*)

☆ Jesus Cleanses the Temple (*John 2:13-22*)

☆ Man with the Withered Hand (*Mark 3:1-6*)

☆ Man at the Pool (*John 5:1-9*)

☆ Parable of the Rich Fool (*Luke 12:16-21*)

☆ Parable of Persistent Widow (*Luke 18:1-8*)

☆ The Widow's Offering (*Luke 21:1-4*)

☆ Jesus is the True Vine (*John 15:1-5*)

☆ The Transfiguration (*Mark 9:2-8*)

☆ The Road to Emmaus (*Luke 24:13-35*)

"Jesus did many other things as well. If every one of them were written down, I suppose that even the whole world would not have room for the books that would be written." John 21:25

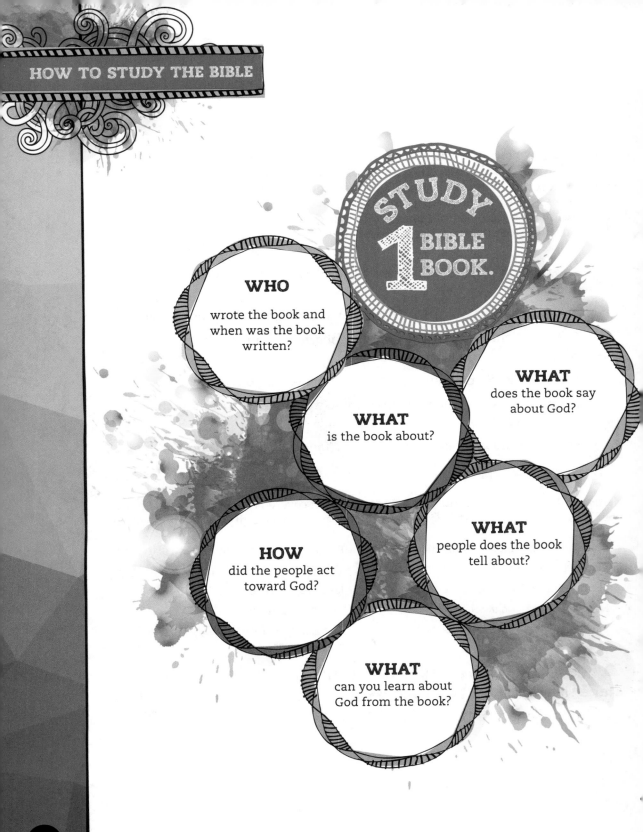

STUDY **1** BIBLE BOOK.

WHO wrote the book and when was the book written?

WHAT is the book about?

WHAT does the book say about God?

WHAT people does the book tell about?

HOW did the people act toward God?

WHAT can you learn about God from the book?

STUDY 1 BIBLE VERSE.

READ the verse from different Bible translations.

WHAT are the important words in the verse?

WHAT are the words you don't understand?

WRITE the verse in your own words. What can you learn from the verse?

STUDY 1 PERSON.

WHEN and where did the person live?

WHAT took place in the person's life?

HOW did the person act?

WHAT can you learn from the person?

THE GOSPEL:
God's Plan for Me

The word gospel means "good news." It is the message about Christ, the kingdom of God, and salvation.

 GOD RULES. The Bible tells us God created everything, including you and me, and He is in charge of everything. Invite a volunteer to recite Genesis 1:1 from memory or read it from his Bible. Read Revelation 4:11 and Colossians 1:16-17.

 WE SINNED. Since the time of Adam and Eve, everyone has chosen to disobey God (Romans 3:23). The Bible calls this sin. Because God is holy, God cannot be around sin. Sin separates us from God and deserves God's punishment of death (Romans 6:23).

 JESUS GIVES. Read John 3:16 aloud. God sent His Son, Jesus, the perfect solution to our sin problem, to rescue us from the punishment we deserve. It's something we, as sinners, could never earn on our own. Jesus alone saves us. Read Ephesians 2:8-9.

 GOD PROVIDED. Jesus lived a perfect life, died on the cross for our sins, and rose again. Because Jesus gave up His life for us, we can be welcomed into God's family for eternity. This is the best gift ever! Read Romans 5:8; 2 Corinthians 5:21; or 1 Peter 3:18.

 WE RESPOND. We can respond to Jesus. "The ABCs of Becoming a Christian" is a simple tool that helps us remember how to respond when prompted by the Holy Spirit to the gift Jesus offers.

ADMIT to God that you are a sinner. The first people God created chose to sin and disobey God. Ever since then, all people have chosen to sin and disobey (Romans 3:23). Tell God you messed up and you are sorry for doing your own thing and turning away from Him through your thoughts, words, and actions. Repent, turn away from your sin. (Acts 3:19; 1 John 1:9) Repent doesn't just mean turning from doing bad things to doing good things. It means turning from sin and even from your own good works and turning to Jesus, trusting only in Him to save you.

BELIEVE that Jesus is God's Son and receive God's gift of forgiveness from sin. You must believe that only Jesus can save you and you cannot save yourself from your sin problem—not even by praying to God, going to church, or reading your Bible. Your faith or your trust is only in Jesus and what He did for you through His life, death, and resurrection. (Acts 16:31; Acts 4:12; John 14:6; Ephesians 2:8-9)

CONFESS your faith in Jesus Christ as Savior and Lord. Tell God and tell others what you believe. If Jesus is your Savior, you are trusting only in Him to save you. Jesus is also Lord, which means He is in charge and calling the shots in your life. You can start following Him and doing what He says in the Bible. You are born again into a new life and look forward to being with God forever. (Romans 10:9-10,13)